MASQUERADE
An Adventure in Iran

MASQUERADE:

AN ADVENTURE IN IRAN

SARAH HOBSON

ACADEMY
CHICAGO
LIMITED

American Edition 1979
Published by Academy Chicago Limited
360 North Michigan Avenue, Chicago, Il. 60601

Library of Congress Cataloging in Publication Data

Hobson, Sarah, 1947-
    Masquerade, an adventure in Iran.

    Reprint of the ed. published by Murray, London,
under title: Through Persia in Disguise.
    Includes index.
    1. Iran--Description and travel.
2. Hobson, Sarah, 1947-   I. Title.
[DS259.H57 1979]   915.5'04'50924 [B]
ISBN 0-89733-013-7   79-12435

For my mother
Beryl
and my sisters
Edwina and Caroline

Contents

Illustrations

From the author's photographs

AUTHOR'S NOTE AND ACKNOWLEDGEMENTS

I was very happy when I heard that this book would be published in the United States, not just because of the extended readership, but because it acted as a catalyst for rejudging the experience. On the whole, I remember my journey with affection, gratitude, and sometimes even surprise.

The experience changed me in many ways: it made me understand more about myself, particularly as a woman; it made me reconsider my values, and my behaviour within relationships; it set me on a course of documentary writing and research relating to other cultures, and on a quest for the meaning of human development; and it laid the foundations for a continuing involvement in Iran.

I have been back many times both to research and to revisit the friends I made. Recently I spent more than two years working with leading academics on a televised history of Iran. I am indebted to them for the knowledge and experience they shared, and for the understanding they gave me of contemporary Iran.

During these journeys I encountered many levels of society, from mosque, to palace, to village, factory, and bazaar. But the more I see of Iran, the more I realise the difficulty of generalisation, for the elements are so subtle, so complex, and so varied. Iranian society itself is a wide mixture of races, religions, and requirements and different experiences. Even classification according to class and occupation is misleading, for Iranian society is extraordinarily fluid and flexible. It has learnt to adapt to the devastation of history, and to the powerful determinants of geography.

Iran is a vast land—mountainous and arid with patches of fertility. The scenery moves dramatically from desert to forested hillside, from barren peak to dry valley occasionally watered by stream or man-made channel. Intense heat in summer; thick snow in winter.

Once this land was crossed by the great overland trade routes which brought an enrichment of revenues, raw materials, diverse goods, people, ideas, and the growth of cities. It also established a route for invaders, such as the Greeks, the Arabs, and the Mongols. Many alien people swept through Iran, to conquer, settle, and rebuild, turning widespread destruction into swift reconstruction. The history of Iran is indeed the history of invasion and settlement, cycle upon cycle: Iran not only survived such onslaughts but assimilated its conquerors and adapted what they brought—Greek science and learning; Chinese art and technology; the religion of Islam.

Another strand also defines its history—those isolated communities which were protected from subjugation by impenetrable mountain and desert, and which defied central authority whether as ethnic or tribal groups well into the twentieth century. Such isolation also encouraged heterodoxy, and though Iran has been Muslim for some 1300 years, adherence to one particular branch of Islam has fluctuated through the centuries. It was not until the sixteenth century that Shi'a Islam became the state religion and Shi'ite priests were brought in to provide greater authority.

And of course there has been the recent dimension of oil, which attracted British and American imperialism, and which financed a ruthless drive towards technical modernisation while supporting military and royal power.

I cannot claim that this book provides a detailed study of the country, but I do believe that—as the experience did for me—it opens the door to aspects of Iran which have been neglected by observers. It is not a political book, for that was not the purpose of the journey: it was a journey of exploration, of associating myself with another culture, and of trying to understand more of others as well as myself in the context of a landscape.

There have of course been recent and dramatic changes in Iran, but an explanation of the causes would require another book. I have therefore simply extended the story—at least my version of the story—in a concluding chapter in order to give a wider perspective and to provide perhaps some pointers towards the conflict.

When I first wrote the book, I found it a hard decision to include my stay in Qum, for it was an intimate and personal experience which occurred only through the generosity of people there. In no way did I wish to abuse their hospitality by describing them in detail, but I felt it was the best way to convey the insights which they gave me. Nothing I have said is meant to disparage, and if I have misinterpreted or offended, then I apologise deeply. The book is written for a Western audience, and I am conscious that much of it would seem slight to a Muslim or Iranian.

Throughout, I have used Professor A. J. Arberry's translation of the Quran, *The Koran Interpreted,* reprinted by kind permission of Macmillan Publishing Co. Inc., New York, ©George Allen & Unwin Ltd., London 1955. I have used blank verse for other religious teachings in an attempt to indicate the speaker's method of speech.

Language—both Persian and Arabic—was a particular problem in Qum, for the vocabulary was often technical and its usage very skilled. I therefore relied on Hasan-'Ali for translation, since he spoke fluent Arabic, Persian, Urdu, and English. On every occasion I was allowed to take notes.

Elsewhere in Iran, I relied on my own Persian or on students (as in Isfahan) who acted as interpreters. I have not included them in the book for the sake of fluency, but I am grateful to them for their help.

My warmest thanks go to my mother and Carol Whitelaw for their patience, understanding and help while I was writing this book. Also to Colin Thubron who gave much time and criticism to the early stages of the manuscript and who helped me to be more self-aware. I would also like to thank Morton Paley for his lucid literary comments, and Robert Hillenbrand for checking my history. I am extremely grateful to various friends for their encouragement and advice, especially Celia Phillips and Bryan Bennett; and to David Watkinson who printed the photographs.

Finally there are those people of Iran who gave me hospitality and friendship. They taught much, and shared more: it is they who led me into their country.

The name Persia has been known to Europe since the sixth century when the great battles of Marathon and Salamis were waged between the Greeks and the Persians. 'Persia' derives from the word Fars, the name of a southern province in Iran from whence two ancient Persian Empires grew. Fars also gives its name to the language, *farsi,* or Persian.

The use of 'Persia' and 'the Persians' by Europe continued into the Islamic period and developed connotations of specific cultural and artistic achievements—the Persian miniature, Persian mosques, the Persian carpet.

It was in the 1930s that Reza Shah, the new Pahlavi monarch, stipulated usage of the term 'Iran' to describe the political state he ruled—a state whose boundaries had been settled largely by the British and the Russians in the course of the nineteenth century. 'Iran' is by origin the same word as Aryan, and throughout history has been intermittently applied to the peoples of Aryan origin occupying the plateau, and to the plateau itself.

I have therefore used either term in what I hope is the appropriate context.

Metamorphosis

IT IS DIFFICULT in London to buy drab, shapeless clothes which will disguise the shape of a woman and withstand the dirt and heat of travelling. After a day in the West End, I went to a shop in Clapham and found a pair of khaki cotton trousers. I tried them on but they did not hide my shape.

'Don't you have anything baggier?' I asked the assistant.

'They're a bit big already, aren't they,' he said, running a hand over his own tightly bound hip.

'No, it's all right. You see, I'm dressing as a boy.'

He smoothed his hair against his neck. 'Well dear, wouldn't your girl-friend prefer something more *revealing*?'

In the next man's shop, I selected an olive Aertex shirt.

'What size does your husband take, Madam?' asked the man behind the counter.

'Oh, I'm not married. I should think size forty-two will do.'

He winked. 'Handsome, is he?'

'It's not for a man. I mean it is in a way. It's for me. I'm going to Iran.'

A man piling boxes in the corner turned to look at me, but resumed his work with disappointment as I slipped the shirt easily over my jersey.

But why Iran, and why as a boy? I remember vividly a lecture on Persian Islamic art, where the photographs were full of intricate patterns and colours: arabesques swirling through acres of tile-work, turquoise domes sphered against a brown desert, carpets swamped with flowers, and jade-coloured minarets mirrored in pools where Muslims washed for prayer.

Such images summed up my feeling for Persia, for it seemed that its art was a part of religion, an expression of faith, where the artist was seeking perfection simply, yet fully, because his work was God's. I felt that Islam encompassed, indeed was the essence of Persia—perhaps it was comparable to medieval England, when I felt that Christianity was part of everyday life, where its culture and art were inspired by a common imagery and rhythm. Did such a unity, I wondered, still exist in Persia?

I wanted to know more about Islam, its tenets, its philosophy, and to see how it was translated into practical life. I particularly wanted to see it in Persia, for I felt that her interpretation was somehow lighter, more delicate than Arab countries. Perhaps it was the colouring of her earlier culture—Zoroastrian dualism with the Achaemenian dynasty, Greek classicism under Alexander the Great. Perhaps also it was the effect of innumerable invasions, so that she was constantly sifting and refining to retain her identity.

But apart from the meaning, I also wanted to explore the mechanics of design there. A friend and I had a business in London, drawing and making up leather goods. We used other materials as well—enamel, perspex, metal—and I felt if I studied Persian art, I would learn much from its use of texture and colour, its methodical yet intricate patterns. There were carpets, tiles and mosaics to sketch, enamelling and silver-work to watch. And there were also the tribes who, as nomads less imbued with Islam, had evolved their own designs; boldly geometric, with blocks of colour marching across the background.

Finally, why did I go as a boy? From what I had heard, it seemed that as an unveiled Christian girl in a Muslim country, I would experience pestering and unpleasantness. And the danger would probably be greater if I were to visit remote areas in Iran, and holy places where unveiled women had rarely been seen. I felt I could cause trouble, to myself and to others.

I decided to dress as a boy, for though such disguise might not always convince, I felt it would give some protection. For my clothes, I bought the voluminous trousers and shirt, and added some masculine details—a spotted handkerchief, a pipe, and suede boots two sizes too large to make my feet look bigger. While packing an old kit-bag, I remembered other details. I replaced my brush with a comb, and put a razor and shaving soap in a polythene bag together with flannel and toothbrush.

The physical change was more difficult, though I cropped my hair like a boy's, with short sideboards and a parting. I tried to darken my chin with an eyebrow pencil, but my skin itched so much that I had to wash it off. I tried to flatten my breasts with bandages, but they seemed too impractical, and I ended with a wide elastic girdle. In the stomach of my shirt, I sewed a pocket for my passport and travellers' cheques, hoping it would reduce the contours of my chest. Any remaining bulges I covered with note-books in my breast-pocket.

Before leaving, I tried on my disguise, and filled my stomach-pouch with paper. I looked like a pregnant boy.

'Why don't you have a trial run in the street?' said my sister. 'But keep your shoulders hunched. It'll make your front more concave.'

I slouched out of the house and along the street, but no-one paid any attention. I crossed to the local public lavatories and went to-wards the *Gents*, thinking my disguise was succeeding. But the woman guarding the *Ladies* shouted:

'Oi, you can't go in there, what yer want to go there for?'

'Sorry. I thought I was a man,' I said lamely.

'You thought you was a man? My arse. If that's so then I'm a fairy.' And she cackled with laughter.

I decided to hitch-hike to Istanbul to practise my role as a boy, and also accustom myself to different climate and food. I travelled through France in comfort, for my sister was driving to Spain, and she left me early in the morning on the road to Arles.

I waited several hours for a lift, and wished I had a dress on, if that would seduce the cars to stop. But a Citroën van drew up, and a fat man, sunk behind the steering wheel, said he was going to Aix-en-Provence. As I got in, I noticed his hands, puffy, white hands with short blunt-ended fingers and dirty nails.

'Are you going to work?' I asked.

'It's Sunday,' he grunted. I had forgotten which day it was.

'Do you live there?'

He did not reply, so I stared out of the window at the poplar trees which pillared the road, and the vineyards curling over the rounded hills. Suddenly I felt his hand pawing at my thigh. I threw it off, but it came back higher, on my chest.

'Fifteen francs,' he growled.

'What? Fifteen?'

'All right then, twenty.'

'No, not for any amount.'

'But you must need the money. All you hitch-hikers do.'

'Well I don't. I hitch-hike for fun.'

'So you say.' And he turned onto a small track leading into the hills. I asked him to return. He seized my arm. I begged him. He laughed. I tried to take the keys from the ignition, but he struck my hand away. He became angry and started talking of 'la mort'. Visions of a remote farmhouse filled my mind, of being dragged into a room, carved up and thrown into an acid bath. There was no-one in the fields to whom I could shout. I forced myself to become gay, innocent:

'Je ne comprends pas. Qu'est-ce que c'est, ce mot, la mort?'

I could not understand his description.

'But why, *why* do you want to kill me?' I pleaded.

'Kill you?' he said. 'Who's talking of killing? Don't you know what *l'amour* is? O, I see, *la . . . mort*.' And he laughed, releasing the tension. I laughed too, and after extracting a kiss, he set me down to make my own way back to the road.

Lifts were more frequent in Italy, and I began to grow used to my clothes, and to button my trousers from the right. I learnt to smooth my hair with the palms of my hands, and to control my voice to a deeper level. But I could not cope with my pipe. I usually tried to light it while sitting in a road-side *trattoria*. One leg nonchalantly resting on the other, I filled my pipe with tobacco and took out some matches. But the wind blew them out, and I was useless at cupping my hands. If I did manage to light the tobacco, it soon went out, and after several days, I put the pipe at the bottom of my bag.

After a few days also, my feet were heavily blistered, to be aggravated by the size of my shoes. And my arms ached with the weight of my kit-bag. Not that it was very heavy, but the heat made it seem so, and I could not appeal for help.

When I reached Venice, I decided to relax for two days. As I wandered round, the water reminded me constantly of her link with Persia, for both had dominated the great trade route from China to Europe: Persia was middleman, taxing and controlling the passage of goods, while Venice took receipt of them for distribution in Europe. But for both it was not just a matter of passing on the goods, of spices, precious stones, and silk. Venetian

Metamorphosis

and Persian craftsmen translated raw materials into fabrics and jewellery, and the influence of their designs spread simultaneously through Europe.

It was the Venetian merchants who first brought back information about Persia when knowledge had receded during the Dark Ages. Marco Polo gives specific details of its people, its villages with earthen walls, and the legends of the Assassins. In 1324, a Venetian consul established himself at Tabriz; in 1492 a Persian physician's treatise was translated into Latin and printed in Venice; and it is probable that Europe's first playing-cards were printed in Venice because of her contact with the Mongols in Persia.

Both places suffered a setback in trade with the discovery of the Cape route, yet both moved into a highly sophisticated period in the visual arts: the Venetian school of painting and the Safavid revival. Nine paintings were taken by the Venetian embassy on its visit to Isfahan in 1609, as gifts to the Muslim Shah: they included a madonna, a nativity, the Queen of Cyprus, and the Saviour. And when in 1613 the Shah sent his agents to Venice, he asked for decorated glass, mirrors, flower bulbs, and 'masks for disguise . . . at any price'.

Four days later I was interned in a small room of a wooden hut in Yugoslavia. The narrow window, only twenty inches or so across, was barred and a guard stood outside the door. There was one hard bed, a wooden chair beneath the window, and a bare-topped table. My luggage was being examined in another room. I sat on the bed anxiously for ten minutes, twenty minutes, half an hour. Eventually a man entered with a sheaf of papers; he was wearing khaki uniform speckled with badges. He sat down, spread his papers on the table, and began the interrogation.

'Your passport, please,' he said in English.

This was the moment I dreaded, for I had been unable to change the photograph: it showed me with shoulder-length hair, earrings, and worse, breasts. I withdrew the passport carefully from my pocket, and handed it to him. He flicked over the pages, stopped at the photograph and then looked up.

'But this is a girl.'

I nodded. 'I am a girl.'

He studied my chest and face. 'What is your name? Age? Place of birth?' He compared my answers with the passport. 'Why are you dressed as a boy?'

I explained where I was going.

Then came a barrage of questions.

'Why are you in Yugoslavia? What political party do you belong to? Why do you wish to stay here? Have you done your military service?'

'There's no military service in England,' I said. 'Anyway, I'm a girl.'

He finished his notes, and said: 'Very well, you can stay here one night.'

I was thankful it had not been worse, but I realised the difficulties I would have with my passport: obviously I should avoid in Iran all places where it might be checked.

At the moment though, I needed to know where I was. That afternoon, I had failed to get a lift in Banja Luka, and when it grew dark, a young girl pulled me on to a bus to show me where I could stay. We drove to a camp a mile from town, a military camp surrounded by wire-netting where men in khaki uniform were stamping across a parade ground. The moment I entered, I was shut in a room for questioning.

Now the door opened, and a young man escorted me to a dormitory. A girl in khaki shorts who had heavy arms and legs held out her hand.

'Hello, I'm Vesnia. We glad you're here.'

'Thank you.' I looked at her uniform. 'Are you soldiers too?' I asked.

She laughed. 'No soldiers. Communist Workers' Brigade Camp. We come to help after earthquake.'

Over three hundred people, mainly young men, had come in brigades from all parts of Yugoslavia to dig foundations, make drains and start building. The camp lasted a month, and activities were organised by the volunteers themselves.

Vesnia told me to follow her, and we crossed a ditch where some people were cleaning their teeth. We passed through rows of tents until we came to the parade ground: pop music blared through loudspeakers and figures danced between spotlights. A man grabbed the microphone, and made an announcement: 'Spasič

Radomir is to read his own poem, called "Love in a Wheel-barrow".' Cheers welcomed the youth as he climbed on a chair. Vesnia translated his words.

'I fill the barrow with earth. You wheel it away. I watch your strong body, earth born beauty. Cry out for help. I am right here; let me unload it, load you with my love.'

She did not know the English words for the rest of the poem, and from what I could see of his gestures, I think she was relieved.

When we were in our bunks, I asked Vesnia what time they got up in the morning.

'About five. How long you are staying?'

'The officer said one night.'

'But you must stay longer. Will you?'

I very much wanted to stay, but I was not even half-way to Iran. But I thought it would be useful as well, to study closely so many boys and their movements. My own gestures and reactions were still too feminine.

The next morning, I met the rest of Vesnia's brigade when we lined up at half-past five. She explained that I was a girl, and several of them whistled sarcastically. But the leader called them to order and began reading a list.

'Divna Lukič in charge of food for this morning; Dimitri Milosav, repair of the tent; Čarli, you were drunk last night and jumped on my bed. You broke the springs. Make sure you mend them.'

'What about the lavatories?' someone called.

'What about them?'

'They're disgusting.' They were, but it was hardly surprising as there were only ten in the camp.

'If the cleaners don't come today, our brigade will do it,' said the leader.

An unenthusiastic murmur ran down the line. But the brigade did clean them that evening, with no reminder.

After breakfast, we marched in a crocodile down the slope of the camp onto the main road, red banners waving. A boy cycled past with a bunch of carnations, and continued empty-handed as the flowers were thrust in the hair of three girls and myself. After a mile or so of singing, we turned onto a potholed track. People came out of crumbling houses to watch us pass: the banners moved drunkenly, the singing grew more boisterous, and the crocodile developed into a hippopotamus. We climbed a steep slope where debris and orchards intermingled, and we threw down our spades near the site. It was the foundations for a house, dug several feet already, and I think we hoped to dig another foot all over.

'Come on now,' said the leader. 'Get down to work, and no messing about.' He placed himself comfortably in the shade of a tree with his girlfriend, and we jumped down into the hollow. The men wielded pickaxes, their muscled arms driving them into the earth, while the girls shovelled the loosened soil into wheelbarrows with long-handled spades. Both men and women wheeled the barrows out of the pit to empty them, and within an hour, the men had removed their shirts to reveal brown backs already running with sweat. Within two hours, everyone had stripped down to trunks and bikinis.

'Hey, Sarah,' called one to me, 'why don't you take off your shirt?'

'I'm not very hot yet, thanks,' I answered, resenting the clothes I had imposed on myself as the sweat trickled down beneath my elastic girdle. I shovelled another load of earth with aching arms: it was not even nine o'clock, and the sun was growing hotter. I could feel it burning through me in that airless hollow, until my work grew slower and I stopped to lean on my spade and watch the others.

The girls were almost as muscular as the men, with broad backs and dumpy legs. They were nearly as masculine too, in the way they worked. Legs astride, inflexible, they moved their spades not just with their arms, but with the whole of the strength of their backs. It was the details which differentiated them: the light movements of their heads when they talked, the use of fingers, not their forearms, to wipe the sweat from their faces.

I studied the boys. One wiped his hands on his chest with long, slow movements; another stood waiting for the wheelbarrow to be filled, his left foot resting on the handle, an arm swinging gently at his side. None of the boys bothered to replace their hair when it swung forward over their eyes—the girls tied theirs back with rubber bands. And when they moved onto the surrounding ledge of the hollow, the boys sprung up without using their hands, and the girls scrambled up on their knees.

Someone went to draw a jar of water from a nearby well, others picked apples and distributed them. As the work grew slower, the bantering increased.

'Hey Grandfather'—this addressed to a twenty-two year old homosexual with grey streaks in his hair and no front teeth—'how would you like Sarah as your new boyfriend?'

'I'd like him a lot, but when I got down to it, I'm afraid she wouldn't suit.'

There was a building overlooking the site which was inhabited by spastics and mental patients. Čarli, who had been studying his name on his plimsolls, suddenly went up to one who was walking nearby. Every time the man twitched, so did Čarli, but twice as hard; every time the man's head lolled forward, so did Čarli's. The spastic was delighted and tried to hug him, so Čarli hugged him back.

Halfway through the morning, we stopped for a break and each received some yoghourt, cheese and stale bread. Čarli produced a bottle of *slivovič*, and we lay drinking under a plum tree.

'What did you do with your breasts, Sarah?' he asked, drunkenly.

'I cut them off.'

'Did you throw them away?'

'No, they're in the deep freeze.'

But the alcohol made the heat seem worse, and did little to ease the pain of blisters. The skin of my hands was sticking to the spade's wooden handle, and moving backwards and forwards as I tried to dig. I could feel the water gathering beneath the surface of the skin, but only when a blister burst did I examine my hands. Six blisters bulged across my palms and fingers like unripe plums, so I ran to the girl in charge of first aid, who spread ointment over them and bound my hands in bandages. Most of the brigade were bandaged too, but they seemed oblivious to pain.

I spent several days at the camp, and each morning we went to dig, as a separate and competitive band. But when we returned to camp, we were once more part of a community where there was no room for self-praise. Normally I dislike community activity, but this felt different. There was no compulsion to do anything, and even the elected leaders advised rather than commanded. It was the unity and the desire to help constructively that I found stimulating.

This Boy Scout type of attitude seems old-fashioned in England, but there was participation without piety, and enjoyment was spontaneous.

By the end of my stay, I was beginning to feel more confident, for I had practised several masculine gestures, and now used them almost without thinking. And the work had increased the strength of my legs, so that I strode naturally, and swung my arms more forcefully.

I went through Montenegro, whose jagged mountains and slit-like valleys had harboured resistance against the Germans in the Second World War. Lifts were scarce, and I arrived late one night in a small village: the driver was going no further. I felt uneasy, for the place seemed hostile, with dim lights and incomprehensible Cyrillic writing. Rather than go into the only café from which came drunken laughter, I walked away from the village, stumbling along a path until I came to a field. I unrolled my sleeping-bag on the damp grass and tried to sleep, blocking my ears with my fingers against the sound of barking dogs.

The next morning I woke early. Mist hung at the base of heavily-wooded hills, curving in and out of the gulleys. A pale blue film stretched over the sky, turning to lemon in the east. I curled up, waiting eagerly for the sun to come over the mountains, to dry me out and warm me.

'Cigarette?' said a voice.

I sat up, looking quickly round me: there was no-one. Then four children crawled out of a bush nearby, and stood over me staring. They were ragged, their trousers held up by string, their cuffs and canvas shoes frayed.

Soon a group of people on their way to the field gathered round me as I munched some cheese for my breakfast. An old man squatted on his haunches, rocking up and down. His face was like the skin of a burnt milk pudding, his moustache frizzy and coarse like wire-wool. Grey hair skimped over his head into a peak on his forehead, echoing the shape of his pointed nose and chin. He pulled out a leather pouch, roughly stitched with string, and separating a few strands of tobacco, chewed at them with yellow teeth.

He grinned, and said something; I could not understand, so smiled back. He stared at me.

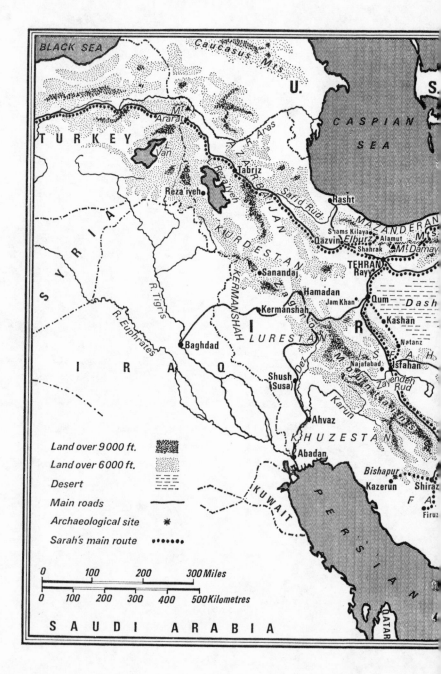

BLACK SEA

Caucasus Mts

U.

CASPIAN
SEA

Mt.
Ararat

TURKEY

Van

R. Aras

ZARBAIJAN

Safid Rud

Rasht

MAZANDERAN

Reza'iyeh

Tabriz

Rezaiyeh

Shams Kilaya

Qazvin Elburz Alamut Mts

Shahrak M! Damav

KURDESTAN

SYRIA

Sanandaj

TEHRAN
Rayy

Hamadan

Qum

Dash

R. Tigris

KERMANSHAH

Kermanshah

Jam Khan

Kashan

Zagros

Natanz

R. Euphrates

I

Baghdad

LURESTAN

R

I

S F A H.

Najafabad

Isfahan

Q

Dez

Shush
(Susa)

Zayendeh
Rud

Karun

Ahvaz

Mountains

KHUZESTAN

Abadan

Bishapur

Land over 9000 ft.

Kazerun

Shiraz

Land over 6000 ft.

F A:

Desert

Firuz

Main roads

Archaeological site ✳

Sarah's main route ●●●●●●

KUWAIT

PERSIAN

0   100   200   300 Miles

0 100 200 300 400 500 Kilometres

QATAR

SAUDI   ARABIA

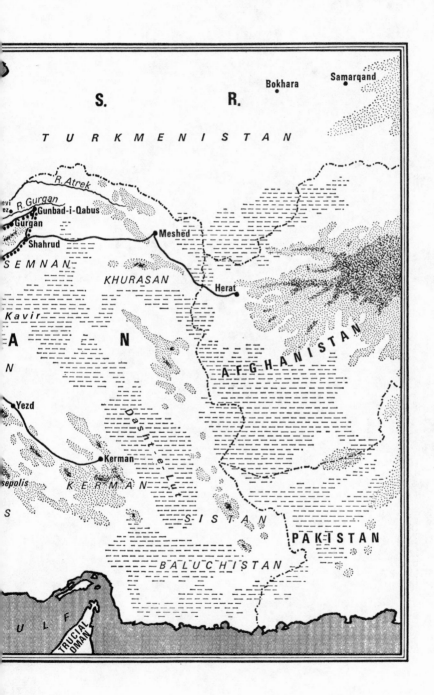

'Hippy?' he asked.

I shook my head.

He pointed to himself, and then with a questioning look, curved with his hands the shape of a woman.

'Boy,' I said, drawing a tree-trunk in the air.

He continued to stare, narrowing his eyelids and nodding his head. I was frightened he and the others might want to confirm their suspicions, so I casually rolled up my sleeping-bag and walked away.

Finding a hollow where no-one could see me, I sat down and pulled out my nail-scissors. I had not realised how much my hair had grown, though it was hardly long, even for a boy.

From Yugoslavia to Istanbul, three French boys gave me a lift. I was put next to the driver, a squat boy with black hairs curling over his arms. He asked my name.

'Sarah,' I said, without thinking.

'Sarah? But that's a girl's name.'

It was the first time anyone had questioned it.

'It's . . . it's a boy's name too,' I said. 'Well, in England anyway. You know, like Francis.'

But he was not convinced, and when he suggested we stop for a swim, I had to admit my sex. And though I asked them to treat me as a boy, they gave me the only camp bed to sleep on; they paid for my food, and refused to allow me to carry the can of water for washing. They even kissed my hand on parting.

In Istanbul, I went to book a seat for Tehran. A bus was leaving the next day, and I decided to leave straight away. The fare was only seven pounds, which for twelve hundred miles seemed an economic achievement; it seemed a triumph when I found the bus was equipped with reclining seats and a refrigerator. But after two days, the satisfaction was reduced by the lack of leg room, and the boredom of travelling fourteen hours a day.

I felt it was a negative way of seeing a country, even scenery, for the impressions were fleeting. White limestone hills covered with green scrub rose sharply from the road like the Cheddar Gorge, then turned into sloping hills of rust red earth. Beneath stretched spaces of cream stubble. Beyond, the land was ploughed in vast strips, its contours broken by stacks of chaff and grain. Further along the plain were villages—a collection of cube-shaped, mud houses whose only amenity was a muddy stream, for washing, for drinking, and for irrigating small vegetable patches. If it was mid-afternoon, no life was visible. But the rest of the day, dogs and geese picked in the dust, wooden carts carried straw to the villages, and men in baggy pyjamas ambled on their donkeys along the main road. Occasionally we saw men and women working in the fields, scything, winnowing, watering, their clothes grey from the dust. Then back came the hills: some eroded and barren, streaking down like uncombed hair, or scattered with stones like a pimpled face. And as my eyes followed the contours, they became heavy with the heat of the bus, and my brain grew tired of the movement. I fell asleep only to be woken by a halt for food.

After a meal, the passengers became more lively. The Turkish driver belched his appreciation and turned to the man behind him, lifting his hands from the steering-wheel to emphasise a remark. An American couple sat erect for hours, staring out of the window, though the wife bent down occasionally to wipe the dust from her white stiletto shoes. Behind them, four Spaniards played poker, swearing and singing according to their cards. A French boy, who showed me the scars on his wrist from attempted suicide, was going to India.

'No, I don't know how long I'm going for,' he said. 'I don't even know where I'm going. But I like to look and see. Maybe I'll find a friend.'

The Iranians particularly interested me. Most of them came from Tehran and had spent some time in Europe. One woman was dressed in French clothes, her hair banked with curls, her nails deep red. I had told her I was a girl, for I felt she would be more open, and as we approached the Iranian border, she began to chatter.

'I love English clothes, don't you? I mean the French ones are beautiful, but *so* expensive. I've got two of their fur coats. But the customs. They're so difficult. Silly regulations about European things. Oh dear, I've got so much. Whisky, tape-recorders, dresses.' She smiled at me, and perhaps forgetting I was a girl, closed her eyes seductively. 'You haven't got much luggage, have you? You could pretend some things are yours.'

'Well, I couldn't take any dresses.'

'But couldn't you say they were presents for a *friend*?' She shrugged. 'Actually, it doesn't matter much. My brother knows the customs men. He said he'd write.'

I agreed to take some whisky, but she passed through without questioning or inspection.

'That was sweet of you,' she said. 'Have you a husband?' She looked at my hair and dirty hands. 'No? How sad. I'm so unhappy with mine. I really want children. But my husband's impotent, I know he is. I've been tested.' She did not lower her voice, though her husband's brother was sitting beside her.

'Couldn't you adopt some?' I asked.

'Adopt? Oh no. I'll have to remarry. In fact, I know several families whose son I could marry.'

There was also a student of twenty-nine, who was training as an architect in Amsterdam. His flabby chest was squeezed into a pastel blue jacket, and he kept scratching his ankles through his white nylon socks. His family had saved to send him abroad, and to pay for his holiday at home; but he talked only of the films he had seen and the number of night-clubs he had been to.

By contrast, the Hajji was reserved, and as his courtesy title indicated, had made the pilgrimage to Mecca. He showed his devotion by chanting long extracts from the Quran, and spent many hours telling his beads. Occasionally he recited poetry, especially Firdausi,* and he stood in the middle of the bus, swaying backwards and forwards, to throw out the words in a resonant voice. He handed round grapes and cucumbers, smiling to reveal toothless gums. And he teased the younger men.

'Why do you wear those tight trousers and nylon shirts?' he asked, flapping his own baggy clothes in remonstration. 'No wonder you are hot. They'll take away your ardour.' And he smiled at his wife. She sat beside him always silent, unveiled but dressed in a scarf and buttoned black coat, her hands clasped in her lap.

We had reached the border on the twelfth of August, with no signs of sand-grouse, only Turkish tanks patrolling the plains beneath Mount Ararat. The customs post was littered with impounded lorries and a queue of people waiting to have their luggage

---

* Born in Tus, about A.D. 940, he wrote the great epic poem *Shah-nameh*, which recounts the history and legends of Iran before the Arab invasion.

searched. We handed in our passports, and sat examining the cracked plaster and torn notices.

You can change your money just here at the first 360 kms.
Keep your receives after you change your money and it is not
permitted to make change from publicity.

Then we were moved into the Iranian sector. Armchairs lined the freshly-painted customs house, the Shah looked down from photographs, and extracts from the Quran reminded us that it was God who was All-Mighty. Officials in neatly pressed suits checked our luggage and made copious notes of passport details. I suddenly thought that if anyone tried to trace me in Iran, the officials might not find me, for they would be looking for a girl. Still, if the last few weeks were an indication, they would not be long misled.

Six hours later, we were through, through into Iran. I walked across the tarmac and climbed into the bus, feeling that the country's character would immediately be different from Turkey. But of course the hills were the same, and the soil; even the houses were still mud blocks, and the air continued to smell of bus fumes and tarmac.

2   *Tehran—Secular Beginnings*

WE PASSED through land carved up by an earthquake, where cultivated patches were cracked and strewn with boulders. Black lumps of earth were scattered among maize and sunflowers and grey rocks balanced on the hill above, waiting for spring when thawing snows would dislodge them. Houses were glued to the face, optimistic that the next set of boulders would again spring over them. They were small houses, light in construction to lessen the damage of earth tremors. To our right stretched a range of volcanic peaks.

Water was more frequent here than in the dry plains of Eastern Turkey. Streams diverged into channels to irrigate fields of beans and vines, and a gathering of people worked every well. A line of trees accompanied the conduits—poplars, willows and almond trees. Villages were numerous, tucked into hollows and guarded by mud walls and orchards. But beyond the cultivation, the hills and gorges were parched, varying only in their height and colour, from beige through cinnamon to russet.

It was late in the afternoon when most of us were dozing that one of the passengers called out:

'Stop, stop, *qanat.*'

The bus drew up and we bustled out. The Iranian men ran forward past a line of mounds in the ground until they came to a place where cold, clear water flowed into the open. Scooping it into their hands, they drank noisily and then poured handfuls over their heads. They washed out their eyes, spat, and started the process again.

Qanat—the oldest system of irrigation in Iran, first recorded by a Greek in the second century, B.C. They are man-made, underground channels which carry water from foothills to cultivable land, even as far as fifty miles. And if the spring water fails, or the *qanat* collapses, the village and fields die.

The water had excited the Iranians, and one of them decided to demonstrate how a *qanat* was made. He took off his shoes, rolled up his trousers, and walked along the watercourse to the opening. Crouching, he pretended to shovel earth.

'*Muqanni*, digger, very clever,' he said. 'Knows what slope to make. Just like that. Allah must help him.'

But vertical shafts, dug down to the depth of the channel, help keep him on course, provide ventilation and allow the removal of earth; and their mouths, like miniature volcanoes, are a characteristic blemish on the landscape.

I looked at the man pretending to dig, and thought of the *muqanni* in a small black tunnel, harassed by falling earth and the shortage of air.

'Worse than mining coal,' I said.

'Better than digging for gold,' said the Hajji, and quoted from the Quran:

> '*It is He who sent down out of heaven water, and*
> *thereby We have brought forth*
> *the shoot of every plant,*
> *and then We have brought forth the green leaf of it,*
> *bringing forth from it*
> *close-compounded grain.*'*

The effect of the *qanat* was stronger than a visit to a pub. Perhaps it was merely a symbol of our arrival in Iran; but for the next two hours, the men danced and sang in the bus, beating time with their hands and feet. A youth drew out a small wooden pipe and accompanied another who wiggled his way up and down the gangway. Even the Hajji gave an enlivened recital of poetry.

Merely travelling on the main road to Tehran, I began to understand the contradictions which exist in Iran, the old and new, the attempted efficiency and its subversion. There were the 'Hiway' police who sat in glass and metal boxes estimating the speed between towns. But the system broke down either because of unmanned checkpoints, or because the drivers sped along, then stopped at a tea-house for half an hour to reduce their average speed.

There were the roads themselves, with impressive wide tarmac crossed by twisting dust tracks and corrugated access roads. Buses overtook motor-bicycles which overtook donkeys. Even the cars

* Quran, 6 'Cattle'.

and lorries were a paradox. A shining Mercedes, its aerial flowing, its new tyres flashing, was crammed with the male driver, two veiled women, possibly wives, five children, four hens and a tea urn. On the roof, the suitcases and bundles were protected not by polythene but a Persian carpet.

The lorries carried the agricultural wealth of Iran—grain, cotton, timber, sheep—or a load of manufactured goods. But they were dilapidated lorries resembling cattle trucks, their wooden frames painted extravagantly in scarlets and sapphire. The drivers were carefree, chewing tobacco as they swung across the road, acknowledging a lorry in the ditch with a wave, and perhaps a grin to Allah for protecting them.

I was unnerved once when a bus overtook us. Its windows were broken and the red curtains flapped angrily against the jagged glass. The left wing was missing, and blood coated the radiator. Contorted bundles were heaped in the gangway, and two men bounced in the driver's seat, their teeth bared in a wild grin, their heads turbanned in red curtain. It seemed more eerie than the skeleton ship in 'The Ancient Mariner', but unperturbed, our driver accelerated and pursued the wreck, overtaking and being overtaken in a cacophony of horns.

As we approached Tehran, the Elburz mountains rose to the left, like up-turned sponge cakes baked in a fluted tin. Their main peak Damavand, almost as high as Kilimanjaro, was obliterated by the haze of heat and industry. Ahead, growing out of a brown, scarcely vegetated plain, was the city, a sprawl of cube houses and blocks of flats.

Tehran has boomed in the last twenty years and carries the flag of materialism. But it has only been a capital since the nineteenth century, when the Qajars promoted it because of its proximity to their native province. Then it was a small town, dingy according to the British Missions, though they were often greeted riotously— Sir John Malcolm was met on the plain by six hundred horsemen at full gallop, tossing and shooting at hundreds of lemons.

As we crossed the suburbs, lemons were still plentiful, piled beside the gutter. Factories also were plentiful, with black smoke ballooning from chimneys, and men standing near the gates hopelessly waiting for work. I found it depressing, for Persian expression, especially detail, seemed submerged in industrial expansion.

Not even the walls of old Tehran existed, walls which had been extended in the 1870's on the lines of the fortifications of Paris. According to Lord Curzon,* and typically of that period, most of the funds sent out from England for the Persian famine were spent on this extension.

I was staying the first few days at the British Institute of Persian Studies, a sedate building protected by high walls and iron gates. And as I was registered as a female member, everyone soon knew me as a girl. Each morning we sat down to breakfast of eggs, toast and marmalade, with yesterday's English papers. Conversation was minimal and specialised—an economist explained with a mouthful the problems of rural-urban migration, or an anthropologist graphed on his napkin the structure of sub-tribes. One or two advised me how to look after myself: I should never go out without a stick to protect me; it was silly to eat in local restaurants; and everyone agreed that whether as a boy or girl, I should not travel by myself.

After breakfast, I went out in my boy's clothes to explore the city. I was disappointed at first for it seemed like any other modern capital with its featureless blocks of skyscrapers and wide tarmac boulevards. Though I knew it to be a commercial city, at least in architecture, I had hoped the Persian sensitivity would inspire exciting buildings which blended Eastern harmony with Western practicality. But according to Sadiq Hidayat, a leading writer of Iran, 'The [Iranian] architects of today despite all facilities at their disposal have apparently lost good taste as well as the sense of fitness.'†

However I soon found reminders of old ways. Only a few yards from the skyscrapers, along the edge of the pavements, were open channels of water for drainage and irrigation. The water was murky and people drank from metal cups fixed to overhanging poles. Along the pavements, merchants spread out their newly-made carpets which swirled and shouted with chemical colours. They invited pedestrians to walk over this garden of flowers, praising themselves for saving people's shoes, but probably calculating that in four months' time, they could sell the carpet as an old and rare one.

* *Persia and the Persian Question*, London 1892.
† H. Kamshad, *Modern Persian Prose Literature*, Cambridge 1966.

Next to a delicatessan, I found a sunken room from which came the smell of hot bread. Three men pulled pats of dough from a large tub, slapped them into oblongs and shovelled them onto hot pebbles in a furnace. A few minutes later, the bread was removed: it was weighed, still stuck with some pebbles, and wrapped in newspaper.

In one narrow street, I noticed a boy combing his hair in front of a shop window, and staring at my reflection. He was wearing tight trousers, and a cream shirt casually unbuttoned to his ribs. Glancing along the street, he walked over to me and touched my arm.

'Hello,' he said, lowering his long eyelashes.

'Hello,' I answered, flattered that he should pay attention to me as a girl in such unappealing clothes.

'You want to come with me?' he asked.

'Where?' I asked guardedly.

'To my home. Don't worry, we won't be disturbed there.' And he ran his fingers along my shoulder.

'No, no I'm not interested,' I said, and began to walk away.

'But Mister,' he called. I turned to look at him quickly. 'Hey Mister, what's wrong?'

It was a wry development. I had forgotten, or at least had never considered, that if I succeeded as a boy I would have to cope with homosexuality; and though it was illegal in Iran, I had heard it was commonplace.

It seemed that most people I met accepted me as a boy. Perhaps I had grown more masculine, but probably they took me at face-value, and put down any doubts to the difference of culture and habits. Nonetheless I was surprised one morning to be picked up by two girls. I was looking for the Ethnographical Museum, and they offered to help; when we could not find it they asked me to lunch. With a girl either side of me, we walked along the street passing more and more eating-places, and I began to wonder nervously where they were taking me. Perhaps they were prostitutes, though I could gauge nothing from their appearance. One wore a lilac dacron dress and giggled, the skin wrinkling between her nose and plump cheeks; the other, in a short white skirt and printed blouse, had a spotty chin and dirty fingernails.

They queued at a bus-stop, and I had just decided to make some excuse and slip away when a bus drew up and they pushed me on.

We sat until the terminus in the eastern suburbs, and then walked along some dusty streets which were flanked by small brick houses. We jumped over an open drain and the fat girl knocked on a door set in a high wall, calling as she knocked. It was opened immediately and six children in faded clothes jumped up and down in the entrance, greeting us simultaneously:

'Salaam, peace. Welcome to our house. Mother, come quickly, a guest. Please, come in. Are you tired? What's your name? Welcome.'

They jostled and pushed to gaze at me shyly from behind one another; they laughed and whispered until an old woman in a long veil came and pushed them away. Clasping my hand she took me into a room, and offered me a plastic armchair with lime-coloured antimacassars.

'No it's all right, I'll sit on the floor with you,' I said, and we both sat down cross-legged. As people entered the room, she introduced them to me.

'This is my daughter-in-law, Fatima, and four of her children. This is Shirin, oh look, what a beautiful dress. How's the child, Shirin? She's got three, but the baby's sick. And this is my son, he's at school. He's very clever. Yes, you know these two.' They were the girls who had brought me. 'Both my daughters.' She pointed to the plump one. 'Zuhreh is getting married soon. She'll live with her husband's family of course.' Then she pulled the other towards her. 'And this one's Farah. Pretty isn't she? She'll make a good wife, don't you think?'

The girl covered her spotty chin with the veil she had put on, and blushed with embarrassment—there seemed no doubt of my masculinity.

Zuhreh spread a plastic cloth on the floor beside me, and she, the old lady and Fatima sat round it. The children brought in the food —fresh green herbs, bowls of yoghourt, warm unleavened bread wrapped in a rag, a dish heaped with saffron rice and chunks of meat, and a separate plateful of rice and kebab.

'Please, that's for you,' said the old lady and gave me the plate with a spoon and fork. The three women dug into the central dish using pieces of bread as scoops, or wrapped a few herbs in the bread which they chewed for a moment before adding rice.

'Don't you like kebab?' asked the old lady suddenly.

'Very much,' I said.

'But you eat so slowly.'

I gulped down the food, and when I had finished, she piled up my plate again.

'No honestly, I couldn't eat any more,' I protested.

'Isn't it good?' asked Zuhreh, her eyes widening in dismay, so that I felt I had to eat it.

The meal was cleared away and we settled down for the afternoon, sipping tea. With the help of the dictionary I always carried, I practised my Persian and they their English. The old lady dozed against the wall, her open mouth showing blackened gums. The skin of her face was cracked with lines like the veins of a leaf when held up to the light, and her bumpy nose was spotted with blackheads. Once her veil fell from her head to show wisps of orange hair dyed with henna, but she woke with a jerk and hastily pulled it about her again.

The daughters were not so particular when their veils fell open, even if I was looking at them, and they made no effort to cover their bare legs. Shirin came and sat beside me. Her hair was bleached with peroxide, and black roots showed at the parting. The pink varnish on her toenails was chipped, and her thumbnails were bitten right down so that the skin overlapped.

'You must come and visit us often,' she said.

'Thank you, I'd like to.'

'My sister's very pretty, you know.'

'You're all very pretty,' I said, refusing to acknowledge her reference to Farah.

'And you're not married yet?'

'Oh no. I'm not getting married for years yet.'

She shrugged, and turned on the television. The family moved closer to giggle and stare at a production of *Swan Lake*. I looked round the room as clouds floated behind the pirouetting swans. The walls were bare except for an unframed photograph of the Shah, and a sunset picture in coloured tinsel. On a mock mahogany table, plastic flowers gushed from a vase which was moulded in the shape of a naked lady, her hair streaming down to her buttocks. The doors of a built-in cupboard were pasted with pictures of laughing women, their faces coated with make-up. The carpet seemed the only thing untouched by kitsch, for it was patterned with arabesque and had faded to soft blue.

The news came on. The Shah had opened a new factory. Another school had been built in Tehran. Oil production was up on the previous month. The Shah was to visit Isfahan. A jet had been hijacked.

The son turned to me.

'You are Catholic or Protestant?'

'Well, neither particularly.'

'Oh.' There was a pause. 'So you haven't been fighting?'

'Fighting? Where?'

'In Ireland.'

'Oh, of course. No, I'm not a fighting man.'

'But why are they fighting? Surely no-one fights any more about religion in England?'

'They seem to in Ireland. But it goes much deeper.' I reflected a moment. 'I'd hate to kill anyone though, whatever the reason.' That seemed unmanly, so I added : 'I mean, not my neighbours.'

Towards five o'clock, I said I must go, and they asked why. I had no reason, except that I could not throw off my London habit of continuous and organised activity. It took me some time to realise that the best way for me to see Iran was to do nothing until something happened, for such was the way of the Iranians. And within weeks I was happy to spend whole days just sitting cross-legged, sipping tea and talking.

I shook hands with the family, and the son said he would take me to the bus.

'You were wise not to take my sister,' he said as we walked along the street.

'Wise? How?'

'Can't you have just as much fun in England without getting married? You have less troubles that way.'

'Maybe. But it might be quite fun to have a wife.'

We both laughed, and when I got on the bus, I felt like embracing him as a man, for he had given me confidence at last in my disguise.

I set out to study the art of the nineteenth-century Qajars,* for I felt they were an essential part of Tehran, indeed of Iran. True, they were greedy and cruel: Aga Mohammad, the first of the dynasty, ordered 20,000 pairs of his enemies' eyes to be brought to him on a silver tray. But for me, they excelled in the traditions of Iranian sovereignty, its display and aloofness, and represented a secularity not found in the rest of the country. Not that the rulers separated themselves from religion, but they seemed more concerned with kingship.

I spent much of my time studying Qajar pieces—papier-mâché pen boxes, mirror frames and snuff boxes decorated in lacquer. Some depicted traditional scenes of battles or gardens filled with kneeling men, but others had realistic street scenes with carriages and gutters, or figures of upturned women dancing on their hands, their skirts and trousers alive with folds. Still others had floral patterns, some glowing with natural flowers in amber, copper and faded cinnabar colours. There were roses, camelias, tulips, and small flowers resembling primroses and forget-me-nots—all the favourite flowers of a contemporary English chintz. Perhaps it was no coincidence, for English fabric was coveted by members of the court, who made it into long quilted vests or tied it round their tabard-type coats.

In most of these pieces, there was a richness of colour and form which seemed to express the sensuality and ostentation of the Qajars. And it seemed that the style had moved away from the strict traditions of Persian miniatures, to incorporate Western concepts of perspective in depth and delineation. This was particularly so in the larger paintings where figures were set against blank windows, or velvet-textured drapes, more in the style of Italian Renaissance painting. There was even a madonna and child in pyramidal da Vinci pose.

I was also struck by the resemblance to Byzantine facial features. Both men and women had wide heavy eyes, long straight noses, rose-bud lips, thick black eyebrows which usually met in the middle, and hair neatly arranged in curves of recurring lines. It seemed odd that the artists of such a secular dynasty might have derived their inspiration from a religious art—though perhaps it gave them the excuse of disregarding the Islamic ban on human

* Aga Mohammad was crowned Shah in 1796; Ahmad Shah left for Europe in 1923, ending the Qajar succession. He had been Shah more in name than effect.

representation. But it certainly seemed that both Russian and European influence, so strong politically in Persia in the nineteenth century, had also penetrated the country's art.

The portraits were mainly of princes or courtiers, but a few girls balanced upside-down on knives. There was strong use of black which set off the splashes of subdued scarlet and pale mustard, and highlighted the creamy white of jewels—for jewels hung in their hair, on belts and daggers, and were sewn in solid formation along borders, collars and cuffs.

The more I looked at this Qajar art, the more I felt that the contact with Europe had revived an art which had become degenerate, even if its revival was secular and outside the tradition of Islam. Certainly the effects of Nasir ud-Din Shah's three visits to Europe* stimulated bizarre innovations in Tehran: the theatre in his palace complex was given a dome like the Albert Hall; Victorian gas-lamps lit up his rose-garden; and so delighted had he been with the Parisian ballet that he insisted his harem wear the *tutu*, and soon all fashionable women were doing the same.

Later I went to see the crown jewels in the Central Bank of Iran, for many of the pieces are Qajar. I found them spectacular, but overpoweringly opulent. Fath 'Ali Shah's coronation crown shone with hundreds of rubies and pearls, surmounted by a soft plume of diamonds. Candlesticks and platters of gold glistened with emeralds; belts and daggers were impossibly heavy with so many jewels studding their surface. There was a throne encrusted with over 27,000 stones, and handfuls of pearls and rubies strewn on shelves. A globe was on a gold stand, its oceans made of emeralds, the continents of rubies, with Iran, France and England highlighted in diamonds.

Yet these jewels are not just typical of the Qajars, but rather form part of the heritage of kingship which stretches back over two thousand years. And I felt that though such spectacle opposed Islamic principles, yet nonetheless they formed part of Iran, were an intrinsic part of its character. For with many of its rulers, right back to the Achaemenians, there had been a love of display for its own sake which bore little relation to the lives and beliefs of the people.

* In 1873, 1878 and 1889.

24

I often wandered round Tehran in the afternoon, for it seemed to lose its officiousness and relax into the heat of the day. I found in one dark shop a man idly stirring yoghourt in a huge cauldron which was heated from beneath by a wood fire. He was dressed in green pyjama bottoms and his chin was black with stubble. As the white liquid thickened, he ladled it into tough pottery bowls which he set on a wooden plank to cool. Then he filled a small cup, and blowing on it and stirring it with his finger, he handed it to me.

'Try it,' he said. 'It's only a poor man's work.'

I squatted on the floor and sipped it. It was good, slightly sour and clean-tasting.

'How much do you make a day?' I asked.

'If God gives me the milk, then about forty bowls.'

'And you sell them all?'

'God willing. He is good to me most days.'

'So you earn enough to live on?'

'With six children? We live, we live. And my youngest son comes to help some days. He's at school, you know,' said the man proudly.

'And your other children?'

He frowned slightly. 'They're looking for work. They don't like the idea of making yoghourt. Still, God will guide them.'

He sighed and turned back to the cauldron, scraping the solidified milk from its sides.

Further along the street, I went into a tea-house. The owner was sprawled on a table, asleep, and in one corner, a youth contemplated the floor.

I sat down quietly and waited. The room was hot and still smelt of the meat the man had been frying for lunch. Chipped cups lay by a bowl of cold water and a blackened kettle simmered on the stove. A torn page of calligraphy hung on the wall and below on the floor was a rolled-up prayer mat.

The man grunted, and turned over, slightly opening one eye. He caught sight of me, and with surprise, tried to wake up and get off the table. He stumbled and fell.

'Forgive me, forgive me,' he said. 'I'm worse than all the donkeys of the world.'

'But a donkey does lots of work,' I laughed.

'Oh well, I can't be so bad then.' And he brushed the dust off his clothes, and buttoned up his flies. Then he looked at me curiously. 'Don't you want some tea? Why didn't you wake me?'

I shrugged. 'I didn't mind waiting.'

'Well as you've waited so long, you must have some tea as my guest.' He made the tea and began to cook some meat.

'Please, don't do anything extra for me,' I said.

'It's no trouble, not for a guest.'

'But you can't treat everyone as guests.'

'Why not? I charge some, and if ever I'm in need, then I can always go to a friend. God will look after us.'

I felt such an attitude was unusual in Tehran, but perhaps in this quarter the influence of Islam was still strong—it was the first time since my arrival that I had encountered an implicit faith in the ways of God. And it made me realise that so long as I stayed in Tehran I would be unlikely to learn from what roots this faith stemmed.

3   *Approach to a Holy City*

THE CITY OF QUM is only ninety miles south of Tehran, yet it bears no relation to the capital. It is a religious city, Iran's stronghold of the Muslim Shi'a faith, and a centre of pilgrimage. For generations it has held a reputation for bigotry and fanaticism: I was warned against it not just by compatriots but by Iranians who were Shi'a. It was a 'bad' place; people had been stoned there; no European was ever allowed in the shrine; I would be foolish to go there; I must go direct to Isfahan, as all sensible people did.

I was anxious still to visit Qum, for it seemed the essence of Shi'a Persia. And I specifically wanted to enter the shrine, though it seemed that the only way as a European would be to conceal myself at the time with a veil. I did not like to think of the consequences if I were found out—anger would be justifiable for my seeming sacrilege, but it might extend to violence.

I went to the bazaar in Tehran to buy some material for the veil. At one of the stalls, with her back to me, I saw a girl vivaciously bargaining. She turned her head slightly.

'Hello,' I said with surprise and touched her arm. It was the girl who had taught me Persian in London. 'I didn't know you were home.'

She looked round and stared at me. With a contemptuous nod, she resumed her bargaining.

'Mahnaz,' I said, 'it's me.'

She looked at me again, this time with embarrassment, for she could not recognise me.

I laughed. 'It's Sarah.'

'Sarah? You?' she asked in bewilderment. And then suddenly she knew me. 'Of course. But what are you doing? When did you cut your hair?'

I explained my disguise, and then asked her about a veil.

'How much material do you think I need?'

She assessed my height. 'About ten yards, more, possibly.

27

You're tall.' And when we had bought it, she asked, 'Would you like me to make it for you?'

I went to her home that evening, and she hung the long veil over me.

'Beautiful,' she said, clapping her hands.

'Beautiful,' said her family, and giggled.

I swayed the material about me, flimsy black cotton speckled with white commas. It was soft, and when I stood near the light, the veil was seductively transparent—I was beginning to understand the advantages of a veil. But then I tried walking, and kept catching my feet on the heavy folds, and losing the veil from the top of my head. I was graceless, and too tall for a Persian woman, and I felt I would be fortunate if I managed to enter the shrine successfully. I almost decided to abandon the idea, but thought I would leave the final decision until I reached the city itself.

The next morning at six o'clock, and dressed as a boy, I took a bus for Qum. It was filled with pilgrims who were mainly women, huddled in thick black veils. They clutched them round their faces so that only their eyes were showing, and when I entered the bus, they immediately lowered their heads. There was a vacant seat near the front—the only one I could see—beside a woman and child. But as I sat down, the women began to screech. The driver hurried to me, took me by the arm and bustled me to the back of the bus where I was squeezed between two men. A male, and an infidel at that, must obviously not defile the gaze of such a holy and feminine bus-load.

As we passed through the southern suburbs, the roads and pavements were already busy with people going to work. But then the houses and crowds ended abruptly, as though cut by a guillotine, and we were on the plain surrounding Tehran, where small flocks of sheep raised soft streamers of dust. I turned to look through the back window and saw a disorderly, fume-spouting city which seemed oblivious of the crystalline quality of the mountains behind.

Then we climbed into the hills, parched khaki-coloured hills which switch-backed defiantly before they succumbed to the desert. The land grew white and relentlessly hot, although it was only the edge of the desert. And as we drew nearer to Qum, the women increased their wailing and chanting. One old man who sat among them, too old and impotent to rouse any feelings, begged guidance from Allah in the way of truth, and the refrain came back from every mouth. Another called out:

> *In the Name of God, the Merciful, the Compassionate*
> *Say: 'He is God, One,*
> *God, the Everlasting Refuge,*
> *who has not begotten, and has not been begotten,*
> *and equal to Him is not any one.'**

When after two hours Qum came into view, the women swayed backwards and forwards, chanting fervently; and when we crossed onto a bridge which spanned a dry river bed, they cried out at the sight of the shrine. It abutted the river bed about four hundred yards upstream: high walls rose like battlements from the concrete embankment which kept back the flood waters of winter. Above stretched three pairs of minarets protecting three domes—a gold-plated bulb, a pale blue cupola, and a sea-green bulge. The colours, and the sheen of their surfaces, were intensified by the brown mat of the mud-brick walls, and the clutter of houses which surrounded its base.

The bus drew up in the centre of the town and I waited until the women had carried out their children and bundles. I walked towards the walls of the shrine, nervously watching those who passed. I followed the walls round, glancing in through the entrances to gain an impression of dark figures, courtyards and tilework; but each time, a man who was guarding the doorway, dressed like a serjeant-at-arms with peaked hat and mace, moved to the centre to bar my way.

I did not linger, for I kept remembering a verse from the Quran:

> *But fight them not by the Holy Mosque*
> *until they should fight you there;*
> *then, if they fight you, slay them—*
> *such is the recompense of unbelievers—†*

From what I had heard, the slightest provocation would rouse the pilgrims to fight me.

---

* Quran, 112 'Sincere Religion'.
† Quran, 2 'The Cow'.

I stopped at a tea-house which looked onto the shrine, and began to feel more courageous. After all, no-one had stopped me, and few had bothered to look at me. And now there was time to study the shrine, though only the domes and minarets were visible above the walls. Nearest me was a squat call-tower, octagonal and patterned with umber rosettes; behind, two slim minarets guarded the golden dome, their bodies seared by jagged lines of washed-out blue and cream mosaic; to the left was another pair, their turquoise surface interrupted by white medallions.

When I began to explore the surrounding streets, I kept turning to look at the shrine, as though hypnotised. Its dazzling colours and multifarious contours seemed in keeping with the bright and relentlessly dry setting, just as spires seem right in the green English countryside.

There were few religious souvenirs and most of the shops displayed *sohan*, a butterscotch type of sweet, made from oil instead of butter, and decorated with pistachio nuts. It is the speciality of Qum, and is piled into glass counters for pilgrims to examine. And in every shop, rows and rows of chrome tins lie waiting to be purchased.

I came to the river bed and scrambled down. Children were playing on the humps of shingle, and black sheep coated with dust picked at litter. A stream—the remnants of a river—trickled down the centre where women were washing clothes and carpets, then spreading them on the stones to dry. The water was brown and fetid, but those who were filling dented cans seemed oblivious to Qum's reputation for impure water. Perhaps they chose to ignore it, for most towns are mocked for some attribute, whether idleness or industry, deceit or over-honesty. At least in Qum, the river floods throughout winter, and supposedly washes away most impurities.

I felt more relaxed as I walked further from the shrine and away from the pilgrims. The place began to feel like a normal town, and not so much like a holy centre. Yet the atmosphere was still different; Tehran is a place in which to display the body and material wealth; Qum is a place for the spirit and the intellect. There are no blocks of offices nor modern hotels; there are few cars and fewer tarmac roads, though orange taxis are packed with unfashionably dressed people. Cinemas, smart restaurants and other places of entertainment do not exist in this city of religion where men devote years to the study of their faith.

Certainly there is a large lay population, some 180,000, but many are involved in the religious activities of Qum. Others earn a living from carpets, the town's main industry. I met one merchant who gave me tea among bundles of wool which still smelt of sheep. He had a long protruding nose, and when he examined some wool, he held it beneath his nose and squinted. He showed me bunches of yarn, explaining which were chemically and which vegetable dyed: browns and beiges from walnut husks, dirty yellow from the rind of pomegranates, a bright red from aniline dye.

In another street I stopped at a tea-house and sat on a carpeted bench which ran along one wall. The owner gave me a glass of tea, and when I had drunk it, a man to my left paid and ordered another.

'That's very kind,' I said.

'It's my honour to help a stranger in Qum,' he answered.

'Are you a pilgrim? Are you visiting the shrine?' asked the other men. 'Where are you staying? It is good you are here. A very holy place. Are you Muslim?'

And when they discovered I was not, their questions gradually ceased and they bantered among themselves. There were no women in the *chai khane* (tea-house)—there never are except in those catering specifically for bus passengers—so each man was able to propound his personal philosophy without being distracted by domestic issues. Such philosophy in this instance went no further than a discussion on the number of kebabs a man could eat without being sick, but at least there was no-one shrilly to ask where the money would come from to buy so many.

Opposite the tea-house was an archway into the bazaar, a dark tunnel lit at intervals by circular gaps in the multi-domed roof. Goods ranged from scarlet nylon pants to hand-woven horse bridles, and each trader tried to convince me that his were the only goods with both quality and cheapness. Behind the main trading area were small passages and rooms, usually unlit and airless. There sweet-makers stirred cauldrons of sugar and oil as young boys bore away trayfuls of hardened *sohan* on their heads; dyers dipped loops of wool into bubbling liquid; old men clanked

31

at brass with hammer and nails. And always there was the smell of spices, of dust and excrement.

Beyond the bazaar was the residential part of the town, the old city. Narrow passages wound between buildings whose high mud walls and closed doors thwarted prying eyes. The thud of metal pots and the muffled voices of females drifted out; it was midday, and the only person I saw was a woman in a narrow alley: she drew her veil round her tightly, stood with her face to the wall and waited until this European boy was out of sight.

The blank walls and skyline were monotonously regular, broken only by an occasional door and wind-towers. The towers were square with four sunken openings at the top to catch the breezes for air-conditioning. They were made of sun-baked mud and crooked poles, but were lavishly decorated in Gothic style. I had little sense of direction among such a labyrinth of passages, and I had to refer to the sun and the position of shadows for guidance.

By chance I came to a mosque, whose recent restoration gave it, I felt, a rather clinical air. But opposite its entrance was a stone archway with steps leading down to a heavy wooden door. The door was open, and seeing a courtyard and tilework within, I presumed it was part of the mosque. As I entered, I saw some robed figures wandering to and fro, chanting verses from the books they held. It was a *madraseh*, a theological college, and not wishing to intrude, I turned to leave. A figure near the doorway called to me in Persian:

'Peace be upon you, and the blessings of God.'

'And peace to you all,' I replied.

'Come, refresh yourself here. Sit down in the shade, and I'll fetch some water.'

I walked over and sat beside him on the stone floor. Round the courtyard zigzagged a low building indented with arched recesses. Off these led small rooms, their entrances covered with white cotton curtains, static in the draughtless heat. The sun beat down on a central pool surrounded by pomegranate and fig trees; an old man shuffled round watering the tiny beds of flowers. It was peaceful and the motion and murmuring of the robed figures added to the tranquillity.

'We pick the pomegranates on a Friday,' said the man beside me. I did not like to ask whether the fruits of God were distributed

on a Friday because it was His day, the day of rest, or more prac-
tically because it was the only time the students were together.

'But you speak English!' I said.

'Praise to God,' he said. 'I speak Arabic and Urdu as well.
Should we not understand the words of our fellowmen? But most
importantly, should we not understand the words of the Messenger
of God, our Holy Prophet Mohammad?'

He was a large man: not tall, but heavily built with broad
shoulders held well back. Two incisive streaks ran from the side
of his nostrils to the edge of his mouth, and a black beard formed a
sharp 'W' on his chin. He was unturbanned, his head closely
shaven, and a collarless white shirt showed at his neck beneath
his brown robes.

'And you've learnt all your languages in Qum?'

'No, I spent some years in India. And I've travelled, to study
and to visit the holy places. But I've never been further west than
Jerusalem.'

'Jerusalem? The Haram es-Sherif?'

'You have been there? You have been to the place where our
prophet ascended to Heaven?'

I nodded.

'Did you make a pilgrimage? Over what festival?

'I'm afraid I was there over Easter. I mean not specifically—
I'm not very good for any sort of pilgrimage.'

'Of course,' he said. 'For a moment, I thought you might be
Muslim. Still,' he laughed, 'you have come to Qum, and that
surely is a sign.' He stood up. 'But I don't even know your name.
Mine's Hasan-'Ali.'

'And I'm John.'

'Then welcome, John.'

We shook hands.

'Well, John, if it pleases you, let's go to my room where it's
cooler. Then we can talk in peace.'

He seemed to accept without question that I was a boy, so I
stood up and we went across the courtyard to one of the small
rooms.

I entered first and then turning to see Hasan-'Ali remove his
heel-less slippers, I returned to do likewise. The room was twice
the width of a low bed which lay in one corner, and only a little

longer. To the left of the door was a small window with a deep ledge where cooking pots were piled, paper bags of spices and tea, and some unleavened bread folded into four. On the floor nearby stood the *samovar*, a tea urn of chrome, on which an enamel teapot squatted. The white-washed walls were lined with books, both hardback and paperback: philosophical and religious works in Arabic, poetry and more philosophy in Persian, novels in English. And between them were postcards of the shrines at Najaf and Kerbela, and portraits of the holy leaders.

Hasan-'Ali pulled out some photographs from a trunk and handed them to me. 'The Imams' shrines in Iraq,' he explained. 'I've just made a pilgrimage there—it's one of the duties of a Muslim, pilgrimage, you know. Of course the greatest pilgrimage is to Mecca. It is wonderful, these shrines. To think I was so near our holiest men!'

These Imams, or leaders, form one of the basic differences of belief between the Sunni and Shi'a Muslims. The Sunnis, who comprise three-quarters of the Muslim world, claim that the rightful successors to the prophet Mohammad were those elected by the leaders of the people, with Abu Bakr as the first leader. The Shi'as argue that Mohammad's successors were appointed by God and that His will was transmitted through the Prophet and thereafter only through members of his family. According to the Shi'a faith, the Imams number twelve: no-one has succeeded the Twelfth for he is alive still, though hidden.

Hasan-'Ali poured out a glass of tea, and placed a bowl of pistachio nuts beside me. We sat cross-legged facing each other.

'Have you some faith then, John?' he asked.

'I'm not sure. Yes, I think so, but it's vague. And I'm often sceptical.'

'Why? How did you come to doubt? When you look at a flower, or delicious fruits, or a sunny clear morning, don't you feel the presence of God?'

We talked through the afternoon about God, our families and the Olympic Games; we drank tea and chewed nuts, and for minutes we would sit in silence, thinking over the words of the other. Students came into the room at frequent intervals to greet me, look at me and ask questions. Where was my faith? Where did I think God was then? Not that He would mind—He had quite enough to think about. But I must be seeking if I was in Qum. That was good. They were glad. One man quoted from the Quran: *He that seeks guidance shall be guided to his own advantage, but he that errs shall err at his own peril.* Others laughed at my arguments, but none condemned them; they put forward their own views and always listened to my answers.

After several hours, I became uncomfortable and shifted my legs beneath me. Hasan-'Ali remained motionless in the middle of the room, his brown robes spread about him.

'I'm sorry,' I apologised. 'I'm not used to sitting like this.'

He laughed. 'Don't worry. A bit of good practice and you'll sit for hours. Then see if God's influence doesn't straighten your back.'

I automatically put back my shoulders, forgetting why I kept them slouched. Hasan-'Ali looked at my chest. Quickly I changed my position and crossed my arms in front of me.

'You do your lungs bad damage, sitting like that,' he said.

'Maybe, but it's what I'm used to.' I suddenly felt unsure of myself, and totally alone. I was defying all the principles of this male sanctuary—no woman ever entered it, I had learnt, not even to cook or clean. I stood up and went to the door.

'I think I'd better go, Hasan-'Ali. It's getting dark, and I've got to find somewhere to sleep.'

'What worries you?' he asked. 'When we finish our discussions, and it's time to sleep, then you can sleep here. You're my guest, a friend, so how can you leave? Do you wish to leave the protection of this good place of God's? Come, sit down again and take some tea. We must talk some more of God's rules, regulations and laws which are the real facts of life. Then you can judge for yourself if they make sense. Didn't you learn at school that two plus two makes four? Then you can recognise that no number can take the place of total four. Islam is the sweetest religion, like the song of a nightingale, for all to hear. But the reality of religion is nothing other than moral human codes. It guides you and shows you how to live properly, saving you from harmful things and showing you beneficent things.'

He continued to talk, always expressing his love for God and the reality of Islam, pointing out that it provided guidance for every aspect of life, from politics to prayer, charity to commerce. But suddenly he stopped.

'You're growing tired, John,' he said.

'No, I'm all right.'

'I'm sorry, I'd forgotten. You're not used to this sort of talks.' He smiled. 'Have we sent your legs to sleep, and now your mind? Let us wake them up. I have to go into the centre of town to see some friends.'

The day was a holiday commemorating the victory in 1953 of the Shah over Mosaddeq. I remembered that Tehran had been decorated with flags and portraits of the Shah, but in Qum there were no signs of the festival. Indeed many people were still working, including a carpet merchant we visited. He was sorting out wools for weavers who worked at home.

His hands were wide and hairs ran along the back of his fingers to carefully manicured nails. He was squatting on the floor, his trousers hitched up to show white ankles above highly-polished shoes.

'Greetings,' he said, 'and the peace of God. Please, why not look round, just while I finish this sorting? Our designer's over there.'

A young man was tracing part of a pattern onto a sheet of graph paper. He made a few changes to a petal or leaf, then filled in the flowers and twirls with bright colours.

'Is this the size that appears on the carpet?' I asked.

'Exactly the same,' he grunted.

'And is it your own design?' I asked with admiration.

He looked surprised. 'No, why should it be? It's a traditional design. We often reproduce it.' Then he added: 'But of course I've made this one very original. Look. The border here is different, and I've made up all the colours myself.'

The merchant came over. 'Fine work, isn't it? Now come and look at this carpet.' He sorted through a pile in the corner, and pulled out a carpet intricately patterned in cream and navy. 'It's finer than the best work in Kashan,' he said proudly.

Kashan is a neighbouring town which produced superb Persian carpets in the sixteenth century. Now the towns rival each other, though outsiders condemn both: 'Kashan and Qum are cursed— see how the one has impure water and the other scorpions.'

The merchant then took me down some steps into a dark room where two men were weaving a carpet some six feet by ten.

'Do you want to try?' asked one as I peered to see what they were doing.

'Oh yes please.'

I climbed onto the plank which was suspended between ladders in front of the warps. I could not follow their movements, for they knotted deftly, but one man took a piece of wool and showed me slowly. Then I tried, fumbling for the correct warps before winding the wool round. It was worse than tying a fly on a cast, and I kept threading the wool-strand the wrong way. When I had tied several knots, I rammed them down against the weft with a comb-like instrument and trimmed the ends to the length of the pile.

'Do you work in silk too?' I asked the merchant.

He shook his head. 'It takes too long. Anything up to three years. I can't wait that long for my money.'

As we walked back to the main room, he asked:

'But what about yourself? Have you got a family?'

'Yes, in England. I've only got sisters though. No brothers.' I touched my upper lip with my thumb and forefinger as though stroking a moustache. He looked at my hand.

'What sort of work do you do?'

'A friend and I design leather things.'

'Steering wheel covers?' he asked eagerly.

'No, not exactly.'

'Pity, I need one for my car. Have *you* got a car? How did you come from England?'

'I hitch-hiked.'

He did not understand, and when I explained, he must have misunderstood, for he ended with the impression that I was a pilgrim who had walked from London to Qum.

'What courage, what endurance!' he said, raising his hands to God. 'It would be Allah's highest bounty, sir, if you'd take my daughter as your bride.'

I did not take in his words.

'She is young still, but she'd be a dutiful wife.'

I stammered for a moment, and then blurted out:

'I'd love that . . . I mean . . . I mean I'm very honoured. But I'm afraid I can't. You see, I'm already betrothed to a cousin. It's been arranged ever since we were born.' And I moved my hands helplessly.

37

The man accepted my reasons without surprise. Indeed he seemed quite undisturbed by the sudden withdrawal of God's bounty; and on scrutinising me once again perhaps decided that the match would not be advantageous. For my part, I regretted that I had not pursued it further to find out the terms of contract, or even to catch a glimpse of the unsuspecting girl.

My reputation as a walker soon spread, and when we went to pay our respects to an elderly mulla* who was acting as a financial adviser, about twelve men crowded into the small room. I was sitting on a narrow bench, and as Hasan-'Ali related my history, they stared at me uncompromisingly. I had to concentrate hard on my boy's comportment. I sat with my legs apart, my elbows resting on my knees with one hand cupping my chin and the other hanging loosely down between my thighs. I frowned slightly, hoping to give myself an air of maturity. But before long some-one asked my age. It was obvious from my tenor voice and smooth cheeks that I had not reached puberty, yet from the account Hasan-'Ali had given of my life, I must be older than fourteen or fifteen. I did not know how late a boy could mature, but crossing my fingers I said 'Nineteen'. Most of the men looked incredulous, though some—the more virile-looking—glanced at me pityingly.

The question of age was often to come up, but not until Isfahan did I solve the problem. An Iranian friend who knew my real sex told me to call myself *khajeh*, which he said meant shark-face, hairless one. Whenever I used the word, it seemed to convince, but I could not understand why it provoked such laughter. Only later did I learn that *khajeh* meant 'eunuch'.

We emerged once more into a main street which ran alongside the walls of the shrine. Dark shadows of people were passing through the entrances; above, an indigo sky outlined the minarets and domes whose tilework was detailed by the light thrown up from the courtyard and from bulbs on the roofs. I was trying to decide whether it looked like Blackpool or a fairy castle when Hasan-'Ali took me into a brightly-lit shop. It was a confectioner's, selling biscuits, sticky sweets and soft drinks. The owner, a plump man in a spotless white apron, shook us by the hand, calling over his

* Religious man, learned in Islamic law and theology. There is no priesthood in Islam.

38

shoulder for someone to bring some refreshments. When they arrived, he sampled a biscuit and said:

'Yes, these are fresh. Please eat at my expense. We like new-comers in Qum.'

I thanked him, and Hasan-'Ali said: 'This man, he's a famous muezzin. He calls men to prayer here. And you should hear the recordings of his voice. They're used all over Iran.'

The man laughed. 'God's voice always goes far. But He's kind. I only have one minaret to climb.'

At our request, he demonstrated his call *sotto voce*—if such a thing is possible for a muezzin. It was penetrating, a sort of wail charged with disciplined emotion.

Outside again, we followed the walls of the shrine, where Fatima is buried.

'Who was Fatima?' I asked Hasan-'Ali.

'Fatima—Blessed be her Innocence—Fatima is the daughter of the Seventh Imam. She was a beautiful person, filled with the love of God. When her brother was near Merv, she came all the way from Iraq to see him. But she became ill near Qum and died. May God rest her soul.'

'But why is it such an important place of pilgrimage? Surely the Imam's tombs are more important?'

'Surely. But we have a tradition where Imam Reza says: "Whoever visits the shrine at Qum will go to heaven." And do you know *why* we have pilgrimage? Prayers, fasting, Hajj,* charity, are the only means of raising man to highest level of human dignity in this world. But they help other ways too. Pilgrimage is the great gathering of Muslims, of all peoples and races. It shows all Muslims equal, in one society, and nothing against colour. Anyway, what's the external whiteness for if the inside is black? And see how new ideas and new science disperse after a gathering of people.'

'But isn't pilgrimage an unfair hardship on poor people, the expense and things?'

'No, for Holy Quran says a man can do business on his pilgrimage. I think Christians consider it dirty, but why? Islam says religious life and worldly life are no different. A man has to live so if he goes on pilgrimage why shouldn't he gain for his soul and his

---

* The pilgrimage to Mecca.

purse together? Provided of course that he doesn't profiteer or trade in tricks.'

As we approached the last entrance, to my surprise we turned to go in. There was no guard on duty, so we passed through a brick archway into a courtyard. The base of a mosque stood naked of decoration, its lines of bricks discernible in the dim light. The building was shadowy, aloof, and even the dome threw off a steely glint. In the adjoining courtyard, tiled walls and arches enclosed a small quadrangle. On one side the entrance to Fatima's tomb rose to a golden dome and medallioned minarets. The *iwan** was a honeycomb of gold; the tiled façade twinkled white on a deep blue background. There was light everywhere—huge chandeliers, spotlights engulfing the gold, neon-strips in the courtyard.

Children, turbanned men, veiled women, streamed past us to a small kiosk where they left their shoes before disappearing through a low doorway into the sanctuary. Hasan-'Ali and I stood back against the edge of the buildings, looking. No-one bothered to look at us for they were too preoccupied with their evening devotions. From where I was, the black figures busying round seemed insignificant beside the splendour of the buildings. Yet such splendour did not seem remote, for there was a feeling of intimacy in the small courtyard. Perhaps I felt it because we had moved among pilgrims whose purpose was united; perhaps because there was no exit to the town outside. But much of it came from the regularity of design and colour which poured over the façades.

'Are they rebuilding something?' I asked Hasan-'Ali, pointing to the heaps of sand and gravel, wooden poles and oil drums in the centre.

'Yes, they're always repairing and renovating our shrine. Ever since the Safavis, you know. Shah Isma'il rebuilt the whole shrine.' His cheeks dimpled. 'He must have been a wise man, knowing which things are really precious and sacred.'

It was the Safavid dynasty which first made Shi'ism the national religion of Persia. And by increasing the importance and beauty of Shi'a shrines, it managed to keep many pilgrims, and their money, within the country.

The third and largest courtyard was different again, its sides

---

* Arched portal.

irregular where buildings jutted in. Lines of flattened gravestones covered the floor like smooth paving, and a central pool of concrete was lit by old-fashioned lamp-posts. Groups were spread through the courtyard: four mullas conversing, a family squatting on the ground, some men performing their ablutions, tribal women chattering together, their bright clothes and white head-dresses contrasting with the black veils of the other women.

Behind, commanding all attention, the main entrance to the sanctuary swam with mirror mosaic, dazzling silver in a flood of lights. A Qajar portico incongruously framed the *iwan*, its four slim pillars and upper frieze festooned with swags and garlands.

I felt what can be termed only as awe. The brilliance of the sanctuary, the dark figures of Muslims who moved beneath without frenzy, the gentle chanting of prayers—all contributed to an atmosphere of peace and certainty, the certainty of God and the need to worship Him.

Hasan-'Ali looked at me. 'Do you think our mosque-builders have wasted their efforts?' he asked. 'I mean, if there's no God? But what do you think? Could they have built this without the great inspiration from God?'

'I'm not sure,' I said slowly. 'Yes, I think there has to be some spiritual belief in an artist. But in itself, does that always bring inspiration?'

'Man is the cold animal if he lacks spiritual richness. And can cold things bring warm, living creation?'

After we had walked round the shrine, we crossed the road outside and entered a modern building. We climbed to the fourth floor and walked onto a balcony overlooking an inner courtyard. Three men were seated on a rug, and Hasan-'Ali introduced us. Holding one by the hand, he said:

'This is my teacher of jurisprudence, a profound man.'

'However deep a well,' he commented, 'you see only its surface, reflecting a property outside itself—the beautiful property of light. All our attributes come from God alone.'

It is difficult to talk about the goodness and wisdom in a man's face without sounding vague or sentimental, but I felt such qualities did exist in this man in the serenity and openness of his expression. His wide forehead was as smooth as a bald man's head and the only lines on his face were laughter wrinkles at the side of his eyes and mouth. When he laughed, his mouth revealed clear white teeth, and his eyes gleamed with appreciation. Large pointed ears gave him a mischievous air like a pixie and he showed me how he could twitch them without contracting his face. When others spoke, he listened attentively, and the tone of his voice was gentle.

Hasan-'Ali must have understood my thoughts, for he said: 'He is good, isn't he? And gentle? Shall we call him Jesus Christ? That's no sacrilege is it? After all, Jesus was a man with love inside him.'

Jesus Christ smiled at his name and delving in the folds of his striped grey cassock, he pulled out a few coins which he gave to a passing boy. Soon coca-cola and fizzy orangeade arrived, and he handed them round ceremoniously, to celebrate his christening.

'A Christian custom in your honour, John,' he said, smiling. 'A Muslim accepts his faith only when he is old enough to reason and make his own declaration of belief. But how old are you?'

'Nineteen,' I said without hesitation.

'Nineteen? You look younger, and yet you seem quite mature.'

'I think the death of my father three years ago made me grow up,' I answered.

Jesus Christ sighed, but his mouth was smiling. 'I never had a father. You see, my mother was called the Virgin Mary.'

Muslims do not believe that Christ is divine, but is only a prophet, though their concept of him as a man is similar to the Christian: that he was conceived by an act of God from the womb of Mary, that he was a healer and miracle worker, and that he promulgated God's Word.

'And you've been talking about God all day with Hasan-'Ali?' asked Jesus Christ.

'Not quite, but more than I'm used to. I'm bad at articulating my thoughts.'

'If I can help, I'd be very glad to. My knowledge is small, but if you have any questions, or anything you want to discuss, I'll do my best. Anyway, why don't you come to my house for supper tomorrow night? You don't have to ask anything about God or Islam.'

It was nearly midnight, so Hasan-'Ali and I got up to leave. We shook hands and walked down into the street which was dim and empty. An occasional taxi cruised by in the hope of sighting a tired pilgrim, and when one driver demanded a high price to take us to the *madraseh*, we hailed another. We were dropped some distance away, for the car could not manage the narrow, twisting streets with their gaping holes for drains. We walked through dark passages, came into an open market-place where a one-legged man was guarding water-melons, passed into more alley-ways and came to the *madraseh*.

It was still within and from one corner came the whispered recitation of prayers. We turned on the light of Hasan-'Ali's room, then prepared my bed in the courtyard by unrolling a flimsy quilt on a low wooden frame.

'Do you want anything to sleep in?' asked Hasan-'Ali.

'No, it's all right thanks, I'll stay in these clothes.'

He nodded. 'We don't usually change either. Just take off our robes.' He gave me a jug of water and withdrew to his room to say his prayers. 'Pray to Allah more for me, John. To grant me strength to serve humanity in His way for Him.'

I went through a passage to the back where the lavatories were. They were enclosed individually so I had been able to use them freely during the day. Nearby a cemented cube was sunk into the ground for washing. Because it was dark, and so late, I decided I could safely strip down and scrub myself. I was pouring water down my back when I heard someone in the passage: he turned on a light which shone only a few yards from me. It was probably Hasan-'Ali coming to wash. I fumbled for my trousers and shirt, disregarding my pants and chest-girdle in an attempt to cover myself. I called out that I was just finishing if he could wait a minute. A grunt was the answer, and as I buttoned my flies, I turned to see a white-bearded man shuffle past, his head bent and his eyes glazed from sleep and short-sight.

THE NEXT MORNING Hasan-'Ali took me into the shrine
again, and it seemed another place now that there was colour:
shining azure, emerald, and turquoise, injected with white and
yellow, and highlighted by dull brown bricks. But as before, I
found that the different backcloths of domes and minarets dic-
tated the atmosphere of each courtyard—the gauntness of the
untiled structure to the north, the harmony and protectiveness of
the smallest courtyard, the assortment of styles in the third. And
in daylight, I still preferred the central quadrangle whose colours
swamped the senses: rich blue was decked with white, and embroidered with the lighter blue of an English summer sky and
the tan of autumn leaves, swirling and spilling into flowers, stems
and symmetrical shapes. The patterns were gentle, continuous,
no vivid geometrics or spiky kufic script. And where the sun fell
on the *iwan's* façade, a galaxy of stars—in reality flowers—pierced
a midnight sky.

The main courtyard was filled with people, for holy places are
not segregated from the Muslim's daily life, but rather form part
of it. Children were playing hop-scotch on the gravestones, families
were eating bread and dates, and old men slept in the shaded arch-
ways. As we walked through, a man called out with curiosity:

'What's that European boy doing here?'

'He's almost a Muslim,' answered Hasan-'Ali. Truthfully, for
in Islamic terms, everyone has perforce to be a Muslim—physically if not spiritually—because he obeys the laws of nature. 'Islam'
means submission and obedience to God, and the laws of nature
are God's. Besides, there are no rituals or sacraments which a man
must perform to become a Muslim; he has only to declare, or
believe, that 'There is no god but God; Mohammad is the
Messenger of God'.

'Why don't you take some pictures?' asked Hasan-'Ali. He had
told me earlier to bring my camera.

'But won't people mind?'

'No, surely not. And if they do, you can stop.'

I raised my camera quickly and then hid it once more behind my back. But some boys had seen my action, and came running up.

'You've got a camera,' they shouted. 'Please, take our pictures.' And they lined up in front of me.

As we were leaving, Hasan-'Ali stopped to talk to a mulla and introduced us.

'Did you get some good photographs?' he asked.

'I hope they'll come out. It's magnificent.'

'So you like Qum?'

'Yes, as far as I know.'

'But do you know its origins?'

I shook my head.

'Long before Mohammad, a town was built on the highest ground because of the floods in the area. It was Qum. And then Shi'a Arab tribes came when they knew Fatima was buried here.'

'And why was it called Qum?' I asked.

'A *hadith** says that when the Holy Prophet was ascending to Heaven, he looked down and saw Satan sitting in this city. So He cried out 'Qum' which in Arabic means 'Get up'. Then another tradition from the Book *Behar* says that the ark of Noah reached Qum and a city grew up in front.'

'Tell us what 'Ali† said about Qum,' said Hasan-'Ali.

The mulla lifted his head slightly and half closing his eyes, began to intone:

' 'Ali says to a Yamani boy of Qum—
    Out of this city shall come
    The Twelfth Imam. And He will invite all peoples
        to the truth. From East and West they will come
        and Islam will be renewed.
    Here is the river with the water of life:‡
    Whoever drinks of it will not die.
    O Yamani boy, this town is a holy town,
        there is no dirt in its boundaries and the prayers
            of those who live in it
            are accepted by God.

* A tradition of the sayings or actions of Mohammad.
† The son-in-law of Mohammad and the first Shi'a Imam.
‡ Knowledge.

From this town, the light of God will come forth
and perfumes will scent the air . . .
A piece of land the size of a skin will be
worth five hundred dinars.'

In the afternoon, Hasan-'Ali suggested we make a pilgrimage to
the Mosque of Sahib uz-Zaman a few miles from Qum. We caught
a bus to the village of Jam Khan, then walked for about half a mile
over flat scrubland. Legend relates that Sahib uz-Zaman, the
Twelfth Imam, appeared in a dream to a villager, and taking him
by the hand, led him to this site and ordered a mosque to be built.
So it became a holy and sacred place, glorifying the Hidden
Imam.

As it was Thursday, many families had gathered to spend the
night and the following day in prayer. Those who arrived first
claimed a position in the courtyard by spreading a veil on the floor
and heaping it with their *samovar* and bundles of food. And when
there was no space left, groups lined the short avenue outside. If
they were not praying, women huddled together, enveloped in
their veils like wig-wams; the children threw stones and chased
each other; the men strolled up and down, cracking melon seeds
between their teeth, and talking earnestly.

Hasan-'Ali led me to a small hillock nearby, saying:

'I must go and pray. Why don't you sit here, and enjoy the good
things of nature? Fresh winds make your body healthy. The pearl
of the mind must have strong shells to protect it. Look around you,
John, simple things are often the most complicated. And spiritual
feeling is often found in the very objects of nature.'

There was little to aid the spirit in terms of vegetation, but in
the distance, the hills were changing their colours like a chameleon.
Gold was soaking itself into the gullies and over the ridges, until
deep pink took over, assigning the hollows to purple. Then black
crept slowly up from the bottom, until only the peaks were left,
like pink iced cakes on a rough oak table.

When Hasan-'Ali joined me again, we set off on foot to return
to Qum. We followed a dusty road for a mile and then branched
onto a rutted track which twisted between hummocks of sand. The
hem of his robe trailed on the ground and the sand swept between
his toes and the soles of his leather sandals. We were talking of

46

God, and the picture reminded me of the two disciples walking to Emmaus. But although we 'communed together and reasoned',* there was no sign of Jesus, and the conversation turned to more earthly matters.

'Are you ever troubled?' asked Hasan-'Ali.

'By conscience, you mean?'

'No, by women.'

I was startled. 'A bit,' I answered, but then thought it would lead to difficulty. 'No, not really at all. I suppose I'm too young?'

'I don't see why. Especially in England. All those women displaying their bodies.'

'Oh one gets used to that. Anyway, men are just as provocative.'

'It's not the same. Women are roused less easily.'

'I don't agree. How do you *know*?'

'It's true. Women function differently. And they're selfish. They should stay at home, and let men get on with the real duties.'

I felt angry, but I had to suppress my feelings, for I could not argue without revealing the cause of my sympathies. I suddenly felt annoyed also that I had so often to control my reactions— sometimes I was not even sure what my real feelings were.

'Yes, people twist things wrongly,' said Hasan-'Ali. 'And few can see the light. I mean a real personality is one who can put good effect around his environment and is not affected by bad. Allah loves those whose hearts are pure and sincere with Him and among us. But in this world there is too much seeming purity. I'll tell you a story from Rumi:†

'Once there was a woman. She was very bad because she wanted to kiss her lover with her husband right there. So she said:

' "Husband, let me climb up this pear-tree and pick some fruit for you."

'But as soon as she was up there, she burst into tears, crying out:

' "Husband, husband, what are you doing? Who's that homosexual lying on top of you? Push him off! Push him off!" she screamed. "Oh! how could I have married you."

'The husband looked up, startled.

* St Luke, 24, 15.

† Jalal al-Din Rumi, 1207–1273, was a mystic poet whose long religious poem *Masnavi* has been called 'The Quran in the Persian tongue'. Throughout, he illustrates his philosophy with practical tales.

47

' "But there's no-one here, dear."

' "There is, there is, I can see him. How can you lie so? He's right on top of you."

'The woman jumped down from the tree, and began hitting her husband till he fled up the tree. Immediately, she pulled her lover onto her.

' "Wife, wife. What are you doing down there?' said the husband, looking through the branches. Who's that man on you, you whore?"

'The wife looked innocently up. "But I'm doing nothing, dear. Have you gone mad? There's no-one here. Come down and look for yourself. It must be that pear-tree that makes things look crooked".'

Some distance on, we came to a small stone portico where a stairway led down to an underground cistern. It was pitch dark, so Hasan-'Ali went first; I was feeling my way when suddenly I felt something cold and wet flutter against my face. I let out a yell—fortunately not a scream—and heard Hasan-'Ali chuckle. I lit a match and saw him leaning over a stone basin, his hands cupped with water. I took a handful too, and soon we were both drenched with the icy water and laughing like school-boys. Seeing my dripping face, Hasan-'Ali pulled out a large handkerchief.

'Here, take this and dry yourself.'

'But what about you?'

'Don't worry, I'll dry as we walk. Like the mulla in Baghdad. He always sat in a river, with his robes bobbing about all round him. Then by the time he got home, he was dry and still very fresh.'

We climbed up again and regained the path. Soon we were stumbling between mud walls and mounds on the outskirts of Qum. We wove through a maze of alleys and finally knocked at a house; a child opened the door, and showed us into a room. Jesus Christ was sitting cross-legged in his white robes, faced by four beturbanned men. He stood up and bowed to us, moving his hand to his forehead.

'Peace be with you, John. Peace, Hasan-'Ali. There is peace in our house now that you have come.'

We sat down, and one of the figures began to intone in a high-pitched nasal voice, swaying slightly and brushing his lap with his hands. Another man took up the chant, his eyes closed, his eyebrows pulled together. Then suddenly they stopped. No-one spoke, and Jesus Christ bent his head in thought. Within moments, he began to speak in a light mellifluous voice.

'What's he saying?' I whispered to Hasan-'Ali.

'He's explaining a verse on prayer.'

'And those other men?'

'Students.'

Two of them looked older than Jesus Christ. 'His pupils?'

'No. They just called in to ask him. His good reputation has gone through Qum.'

After some time, the men thanked God for their instruction and stood up to leave. Jesus Christ turned to me.

'Well, John, do you find it strange that we spend so much time talking about God?'

'No, it seems natural here.'

'But God is natural everywhere, whether you're saying your prayers or going to the lavatory. And for that, He gave us figs.'

I laughed. 'Perhaps I'd better eat more figs, then I might find Him more easily.'

'He's easily found, John,' and he pointed to my heart. 'But it only takes a strand of hair over a man's eye to prevent him seeing the new moon.'

'Yes, my hair's very thick,' I answered. 'Perhaps you can help me trim it.'

'Willingly, but there's one thing I would say first. Don't merely accept what you hear from us. Approach it with an open mind and question all things until you see their reason and logic. Your mind and your reasoning are your truest guides, your greatest proofs.'

'But my reasoning is weak,' I protested.

'Maybe,' said Jesus Christ. 'But it will grow stronger the more you question, and your awareness will increase. A child's logic is instinctive, but a man's is made firmer by experience and examination. So let me ask you a question to act as a touchstone. Do you believe that the world was created as an act of God?'

I thought a moment. 'I believe that the world was created by something, but by what I don't know.'

'That's a start, for you don't deny the existence of an outside influence. And Islam shows that such an influence is God, a single Being. I'll explain, but you must stop me if you have any questions or doubts. And please, if you want to make notes, don't feel embarrassed.'

He began to talk in a melodious voice, almost rhythmically, then paused, waiting for Hasan-'Ali to translate, for he spoke too quickly for me to understand.

'The first proof,' said Jesus Christ, 'is the world itself:

'For who can deny that the bounties of nature—
the bringing of rain, the sprouting of corn,
the birth of a child—are the work
and the justice of One Creator?
And a sign for them is the dead land, that We quickened
and brought forth from it grain, whereof they eat;
and We made therein gardens of palms and vines,
and therein We caused fountains to gush forth,
*that they might eat of its fruits and their hands' labour.**

'And in His creation He made order,
that the sun should not overtake the moon,
and the night not outstrip the day.
And He spread oceans over the earth
that the heat of the earth be controlled,
and He pegged out the mountains
lest the land shake.'

'But surely the world has evolved?' I asked. 'And there's no reason why God should control that development. It's like a factory: somebody builds it, staffs it and then leaves it to function, expand and produce.'

'Would a man who had invested so much money leave his factory?'

'Perhaps not, but he might lose interest. Anyway God's not materialistic. At least, we're not supposed to understand His workings.'

'And we don't,' laughed Jesus Christ. 'That's one of the reasons He keeps sending down messengers, to guide us. They're the second proof of God. How else could they produce such wise and beautiful teachings? Look at Mohammad—peace be upon Him:

* Quran, 36 'Ya Sin'.

He was illiterate, yet He gave us a Book which is still unique in its poetry and knowledge of human ways.

'And surely the *prophecies* are a proof of God—just consider Mohammad's guide to science:

'The Christians condemned knowledge and the search
for truth; they destroyed Galileo and cast out
Bacon. And they brought in the Inquisition.
But Islam loves truth, and the Book supports
    the findings of science.
Who else but God could have known
at the time of Mohammad that the winds
carry seed? That plants have male and female
functions, and that the fingerprints
    of every man are unique?

'And God warned us that if we leave this earth,
there will be no oxygen, and He said:
O tribe of jinn and of men, if you are able to
pass through the confines of heaven and earth,
pass through them! You shall not pass through
    except with an authority!*
For he controls the meteors and planets;
and has made matter from thousands
of atoms; and their destruction
    is the end of the earth.

'And Mohammad said that iron will one day
roll on iron, (that is the railway), and
things which are distant will come close,
    (that is through television).
And two of His sayings have still to be
proved: that the sun will grow cool and that
    life exists on other planets.'

While he was talking, Jesus Christ looked at the wall opposite, eyes seldom blinking and his hands unmoving in his lap. And while Hasan-'Ali was interpreting, he watched me and acknowledged

* Quran, 55 'The All-Merciful'.

with a smile my facial reactions. He expounded the proofs of God's existence, and recounted the part He played in our lives. And he counted on his fingers the five articles of Shi'a faith:

'We believe in the Divine Unity of God the Creator,
Omniscient and Omnipresent, an absolute Being
Who exists from eternity to eternity.
We believe in the prophets, with
    Mohammad as their Seal.
And His teachings are complete for all time.

'We believe in life after death, everlasting,
and the Day of Judgment, when God's justice
will prevail. And we accept the Imams
    as our spiritual leaders.'

I was surprised how many articles were identical to the Christian creed.

'All our beliefs are scientifically possible,' continued Jesus Christ. 'Take the Day of Judgment. Couldn't it be that microwaves are recording our actions, thus making the domesday book? And even if we deny our actions, God will know them, just as a man can smell onions on another's breath.'

'But the justice of God?' I asked. 'The Quran is always talking about His retribution.'

'Doesn't a father chide his child if he knows it will help him? And doesn't a father sometimes punish his child if he's damaging other people? Rumi illustrates this beautifully. He tells us of the chick-pea bouncing about in boiling water.

'"Why do you do this to me?" it cries to the cook. "Haven't you paid money for me? Then why destroy me in your pot?"

'But the cook goes on slapping it with a wooden spoon. "Boil on," she says. "It's for your own good, to bring out your flavour, miserable, shrivelled thing. You must suffer tribulation, to lose your present unhealthy self. Then you can become strong, and give nourishment. You grew out of God's attributes. Now you can go back to them, become part of them."

'"Oh wise cook," cries the chick-pea. "Let me boil till I reach my beloved."

'So you see,' said Jesus Christ, 'God is merciful though He may not seem so. And a sign of His great mercy is the freedom of will He has given us. We can do what we like with our destiny. Isn't that true love? At least that's what the Shi'as believe. The Sunnis believe in predestination, so that a man is damned or saved according to God's Will. Now do you call that justice? What kind of God is He who condemns a man before he is born?'

We had been talking for several hours when Hasan-'Ali asked if I was hungry.

'A little, but I don't mind,' I answered.

'But you must ask for foods when you want them.'

'Oh I couldn't do that. I expect they'll come soon.'

'You're wrong. It's the guest's privilege to order supper when *he* wants it.'

'I'm sorry, I didn't know. Shall we eat now then? I hope you're not too hungry.'

Immediately food was brought: platters of rice, a chicken, eggs, stews, yoghourt and fruit.

'I'm sorry about the meal,' said Jesus Christ, piling a plate with food. 'I wanted to give you an English one, but my wife's away and I had to do the cooking myself.'

'This looks like a feast. I'm sure your wife would be jealous.'

'Don't talk about his wife like that,' whispered Hasan-'Ali. 'It's not polite. Say "good family" or "precious home".'

'I'm sorry, I didn't know. Can't I ask how she is?'

'I think you shouldn't. Keep your mouth as clean as fresh mint.'

But Jesus Christ did not seem to mind the reference.

'It's a pity you're not a woman,' he said. 'Then you could meet my wife. I think you'd get on.'

'I'm very fierce,' I said, glowering. He laughed, but suddenly I felt nervous. Was I over-acting? Or not acting enough? Perhaps I shouldn't try so hard. After all, he was sympathetic, and with luck, if he saw any ambiguity, he'd put it down as cultural—I knew he'd met few Europeans. But if anyone found out, surely the penalties would be severe. And there was no European in the whole of Qum to whom I could appeal for help.

We began eating in silence, for the Persians tend to concentrate on their food and converse when they have finished. The Sassanians some fifteen hundred years ago are said to have eaten in silence: even at royal banquets talking was prohibited, so that sign language was used.

My progress was slow on the second plateful, so Jesus Christ began talking, to give me time to eat.

'Whatever you're doing, Islam gives rules to help you do it best. Take food. What does the Quran mention? Fruits, meat, grain— what a healthy diet! And could we have these talks, late into the night, and keep our reason if we took alcoholic drinks? It goes further though, for we have innumerable rules for the preparation of food, some for nutrition, many for hygiene.

'Cleanliness—that is what Mohammad taught. Purity of body, purity of mind. Why bother, you might ask, what does purity do? It is simply to benefit ourselves, for through purity, we reach a higher state, we come closer to the Pure One. He does not give us a code for His sake, but for ours:

> *'God does not desire to make any impediment*
> *for you; but He desires to purify you, and*
> *that He may complete His blessing upon you.**

'And one of the ways we draw closer to Him is through prayer. But again, we must be clean, for do we want to give Him our dirt? And prayer breaks down our wall of arrogance, and acts as a reminder against sin. Let me explain.

'There was once a man racked with thirst who came to the edge of a stream. But a high wall barred him from the water. Leaping onto it, he began to tear off the bricks, hurling them into the water.

' "Hey, stop, stop," cried the stream. "What are you doing? You're destroying the wall, and making yourself thirstier with the effort."

' "Maybe," said the man, "but with every brick I tear off, I get nearer the water. And each time the bricks make a splosh in the water, I'm reminded of its sweetness, its life-giving qualities." '

Jesus Christ poured out some tea, first swilling the glass and saucer with hot water and emptying it into a bowl.

'Yes, we must care for ourselves,' he said, 'both our bodies and our souls. And there are three things especially which make us die young: insufficient sleep, over-eating, and excessive intercourse.'

Somewhat irreverently, I remembered the remark of a woman

* Quran, 5 'The Table'.

in Tehran who came from Georgia, a country with one of the highest life averages:

'In Georgia, we drink, we drink so much, and we make love, yes, all the time.'

Jesus Christ suddenly stood up and left the room. He came back with two plastic pots, one narrow and cylindrical, the other round and red. He asked which I would like, and thinking the red one might contain tomato ketchup, I chose the long narrow one. He burst into laughter.

'Poor John,' he said. 'Only girls and homosexuals choose that shape.'

My male reactions were completely undermined, and I had to force myself to think.

'Why poor? I know I'm not as virile as you, so it'll act as a replacement when I give out.' I flushed and trying to cover my confusion, I touched my ears and said: 'I'm burning my own ears with my lewdness.'

Jesus Christ followed my movement with his eyes. He studied my lobes.

'Why are they pierced?' he asked.

I was even more agitated. I had let my eyebrows grow shapeless; I had kept my finger-nails short; but I had forgotten such a tell-tale detail.

'I'm . . . I'm part Scottish. It's our clan you know. They're still barbarians. All the men have their ears pierced. It's an old tradition.' And I gave a long explanation of the clan system, tartans and Highland games.

It seemed to convince them, but I kept thinking how in my confusion I had forgotten to guard my gestures and the depth of my voice. Had they noticed? It seemed not, for they continued the meal normally, and I was thankful when we resumed discussions, for I could just sit and listen.

'Is there anything you're not clear about?' asked Jesus Christ. 'Please, you must always ask questions, and argue. We can learn from you too.'

'Yes, there's one thing particularly. You mention often the laws and recommendations of Islam. Where do they come from?'

'From the Quran; from the sayings and traditions of the Holy

Prophet and the Imams; from the agreement of religious leaders, and reason.'

'But surely rules for a desert society in the seventh century are no longer valid now?'

'If that were so, Islam would not have survived.

> 'For the laws of Islam help human nature
> and human nature changes not,
> though its capacity may expand.
> And the laws are fixed for all men
> else they change them to their own desires.

> '*With Him are the keys of the Unseen;*
> *none knows them but He.*
> *He knows what is in land and sea;*
> *not a leaf falls but he knows it**
> And if He is All-Knowing, then He
> knows best how to guide you.

> 'And of the prohibitions we have these—
> for it is easier not to do than to do:
>> To lose hope in the mercy of God,
>> to break a covenant deliberately,
>> to kill a human premeditatedly.
> Note the wisdom of God when He told us
>> not to cheat, to steal, to use
>> an orphan's legacy wrongly;
>> to spread hatred, to aid
>> an oppressor, to antagonise
>> a relative for no right cause.
> Nor shall you be proud, envious or heedless
>> of your parents, nor neglect you
>> your prayers and your duty
>> to help others do good.

'And though we have laws,' he continued, 'we have adaptability —to meet the differences of individuals, whether pilgrims or sexual athletes. If he cannot comply, a man must use reason. Take a man in Iceland. How can he pray at sunrise and sunset in winter,

* Quran, 6 'Cattle'.

for neither exist? But common sense and his watch will tell him when to pray.'

While Jesus Christ was speaking, I looked through my copy of the Quran to find a passage where I had some queries. Finding the place, I kept the book open by tucking it under my right foot. When I started to talk, Jesus Christ laughingly interrupted to say that it was no way to treat their Holy Book.

Not even another book may rest on the Quran. Muslims believe that it was copied from tablets which exist in Heaven and that it is the uncreated Word of God—as Christians believe that the Word existed before creation, when 'the Word was with God, and the Word was God'. And often I found when talking to lay Muslims that criticism, in the neutral sense of the word, of the Quran was as offensive to them as the criticism of Christ's divinity is to a Christian. And often if people saw me with a copy of the Quran, they asked if I were Muslim. Despite this, no-one I met in Qum showed displeasure that I had abused their Book by underlining verses in it.

It was now nearly one o'clock, and Jesus Christ drew from his robe a small bottle of scent. Unscrewing the lid, he tipped some liquid into his hand and wiped his neck, his forehead and the whole of his chest. He offered to do the same to me, but I hastily lifted my hand in refusal.

'Don't you like scent?' he asked.

'I'm sorry, I didn't mean to be rude. It's just that in England scent can be a bit effeminate.' I thought of his hand crossing my chest.

'How sad,' he replied. 'It's good to be fresh with perfume. And though you don't wear it, I'd like to give you a bottle. You can give it to your girlfriend. What would you like—a rose garden, the water of the snows, peach blossom, or a thousand-petal fragrance?'

'I wouldn't know. I'd rather leave it to you.'

Jesus Christ consulted with Hasan-'Ali, and they both looked at me, considering. Then they left the room and soon returned with a phial.

'I think you'll like this. It's the most suitable too,' said Jesus Christ.

Thanking him, I looked at the label. Bright pink flowers bordered a turquoise centre on which were the words:

'Essence of Rose Petals. Made in Switzerland.'

I did not dare ask why it was suitable, but at least I was beginning to feel more relaxed—my masculinity had been under strain, but I felt it had survived.

The days which followed were not organised but they followed a definite pattern. I would wake when it was growing light to the sound of prayers and to see Hasan-'Ali standing on his prayer mat, cupping his ears, bowing from the waist to the rhythm of words and then kneeling to touch his prayer-stone with his forehead. The students would begin to move in the courtyard, to wash themselves in the central pool. There were eighteen or so students in the *madraseh*: I was never certain of the number for they came and went without apparent order. Some nights boys were sleeping in the small courtyard; other nights several rooms were empty. And I was always nervous of mingling too much with them: Hasan-'Ali and Jesus Christ had, I felt, accepted me, but others might feel I was intruding.

Each morning one of them went to buy hot bread to distribute round the rooms.

'But who pays for the food?' I asked Hasan-'Ali.

'We do, the students. But everyone gets an allowance from the Religious Institute in Qum.'

'Everyone' meant five thousand students; but if they did not collect their stipend, they did not receive it, and records of payment seemed vague.

After breakfast, Hasan-'Ali put on his turban and robes to go to his classes; he left me behind in his room for he felt I would cause a disturbance. A few times though, I saw the lessons in progress. They were held in the mosques and colleges, with the students inside at desks or gathered in the courtyard at the feet of a preacher. There were men of all ages, from twelve to sixty, and they sat listening or calling out questions.

Classes were voluntary and self-chosen, so that if a student disliked a teacher's methods, he could move to another. He started with Arabic grammar and language, jurisprudence and the traditions, and after a few years progressed to philosophy and logic. Throughout, he was learning the Quran by heart, and studying Persian and Arabic literature.

While I was sitting in Hasan-'Ali's room, I could hear the

students learning, and repeating things over and over again. Some walked backwards and forwards, holding a book and reciting. Some were sitting, discussing and explaining, for the students themselves became part of the teaching system: each one passes on what he has learnt to those at a lower level.

There are no examinations and written work is minimal. Indeed a student is judged on his reasoning, his knowledge and his ability to discourse for long periods without reference to notes. And when he is sufficiently able, according to his teachers and fellow-students, he may call himself a mulla and go out to the villages to teach.

Certainly there were hours of discussion in Hasan-'Ali's room when he returned from his classes to explain some aspect of Islamic theology or practice. Other students wandered in to sit on the floor, arguing, sipping tea, chewing nuts, and joking or telling stories.

'Like the old man and the oak tree,' said one boy to illustrate the rewards of good deeds. 'He was over a hundred years old and his beard reached his knees. One day he was planting a young oak, when the king rode by out hunting

' "Why do you labour so?" called the king, drawing up his horse. "You'll be dead before it bears fruit."

' "Ah, Your Majesty, that's true," said the old man. "But my son will have its fruit."

' "Bravo!" cried the king. "What generosity!" And as was the custom when he said "Bravo", a reward of one hundred gold sovereigns was paid to the man who had made him say it.

'The old man bowed, and said: "You were wrong, Your Majesty, if you'll forgive me saying so. This sapling has just borne fruit for me."

' "Bravo!" cried the king again, and another hundred gold sovereigns were paid to the old man.

' "And it has borne fruit not only once but twice in its very first year."

'Again the king cried out and again the old man was paid.

' "Old man, you'll bankrupt me," said the king, and he galloped off with his retinue.'

If it grew late while we were talking, one of the students brought food or Hasan-'Ali cooked some eggs and rice on top of the tea urn. The room grew hot with the cooking so we wandered round the small courtyard. It was lit by one bulb, but light came from the students' rooms as well. Most of their doors were open, though the white sheet hung down to keep out mosquitoes. Where it was pulled aside I could see the students reading or meditating. The younger students were much noisier. They chattered together or clustered round an older student; they chanted while cleaning shoes or washing shirts and they giggled and teased us when we passed. Then when the meal was ready, we washed in the pool to our elbows.

Among those who visited Hasan-'Ali was a man renowned for his recitation of poetry, and he was soon invited to show the skills which God had given him. But he insisted that first I recite. I could remember nothing by heart, so Hasan-'Ali pulled down one of his English books. It was a pocket collection of Victorian verses and I chose a poem called *Spring's Surprises*. It compared with McGonegall in rhyme and metre, so I embellished it with dramatic pauses, crescendoes and exaggerated syllables. When I had finished, the man asked Hasan-'Ali:

'When's this boy going to begin?'

Hasan-'Ali explained I had read the poem.

He looked puzzled. 'But he's been using his normal voice. That's not poetry. And he was reading. Why can't he recite from memory?'

'It's a bit difficult as you don't understand the language,' I said defensively. 'In fact there's great subtlety in the juxtaposition of words as to sounds and rhythms.'

'Sound and rhythm?' said the man. 'Let me show you how we recite.' And closing his eyes, he began swaying in time with the words, chanting verses in a soft voice, raising and lowering the pitch with a series of quivers, and expressing the meaning with gestures of his face and hands. It was a long poem, and throughout, the roomful of people swayed also, and mouthed the words simultaneously.

One day Hasan-'Ali and I returned to his room to find a visitor stretched out on the floor asleep. Hasan-'Ali woke him and they embraced with glee—they had not seen each other for months. He was a swarthy man, with a quiet voice, his words evenly spaced. He could not hide his dislike of the British, whom he said had damaged Iran with imperialism. Then he stopped and apologised. A few days later I received an invitation to his wedding, to be held in three months' time. The pink card was overprinted in gold with the words:

In the Name of God
Under the protection of Imam Asr★
Mr. 'Ali Asghar with Miss Husaini
celebrate the beginning of a new life
And for this reason we would ask the pleasure
of your company

Hajji   Hajji
Mohammad 'Ali   Sayyid Husaini

In the middle of the card was a picture of a butterfly hovering round the flame of a dripping candle.

Shah Latif wrote a poem on this mystical image, of unity and ecstasy:

Callest thou thyself a moth?
Then turn not back at the sight of fire.
Enter into the light of the Supreme
And be thou the illumined.

Ask of the moth! What it is to burn.
They hurl themselves into fire,
The flames of love have pierced their lives.

Callest thou thyself a moth!
Come, put out this fire.
Fire has burnt many,
Burn thou this fire!†

There was also a man who always joined in the discussions, for his room was adjacent to Hasan-'Ali's. He came from Kashan, Qum's rival town, so teased the other students:

'The dogs of Kashan are better, far better, than the notables of Qum.'

'Ah,' said Hasan-'Ali. 'But the people of Kashan, *they* are lower than dogs.'

★ The Twelfth (Hidden) Imam.
† Sufi Azizallah Khan al-Zahidi, *Selections from the Sufi Poems*, No. 1 Shah Latif, London 1972.

He laughed, his whole body shaking. He was a large man with crumpled grey trousers which barely covered his belly. He would intertwine his thin legs and remain for hours in the same position like a meditative Buddha. But he was a jolly Buddha, telling jokes and laughing, and when he wanted to think, he would pick up a cigarette, and suck it, unlit, as though he were smoking.

I met many people, for Hasan-'Ali took me wherever he went. A white-haired man with drooping eyelids was the son of an illustrious Shi'a scholar. He was tired of the fame which had been transferred to him and of the expectancy of his wisdom. He wanted to be a labourer, to go to Europe and work on a farm. Money did not matter so long as he could work with the earth or with animals. Could I help, asked his friends, for they wanted to help him? Of course it was right that he should leave Qum; only he knew what was best for him.

There was also the man of twenty-five who was a teacher of logic and whose hobby was mathematics. Gaunt-faced, he produced trays of sweets and biscuits while asking about universities and mathematics in England. His fingers were constantly moving, to twist the fabric of his robes, to smooth his forehead, or break some sugar lumps. At one moment I stretched out a leg to ease it. The conversation ceased abruptly.

'John, don't do that,' said Hasan-'Ali.

'Do what?'

'Point your leg at someone. It's very insulting.'

I hastily tucked it under me again and apologised. But for some time after there was a feeling of uneasiness between my host and myself.

Wherever we went, I felt secure in the company of Hasan-'Ali. The fact that he was robed and turbanned seemed to give me the approval of those we met, and wherever we went, he paid all expenses, despite my protestations. Once, in his room, he took from his trunk a bundle of pound notes which he thrust in my pocket. When I refused to accept them, he insisted; when I still refused, he said I would soon give to someone else and the giving would in turn reach him again.

He took me one day to the Religious Institute, the administrative, educational and research centre of Qum. We went into a small room to meet an Indian who spoke English.

'It is great pleasure which you come here,' he said with a smile, showing neat teeth above a short black beard. 'We have great many boys come to Qum. Already there are Persian, Arab, Indian, Pakistani, Afghanistan. And now,' he flapped a letter, 'we have Japan who ask to come. But you study here? No? What terrible pity, you could learn me better English.'

As I was a visitor, he insisted we have dinner at his house. He was a jovial man with a loud laugh and his words lacked the elaborateness of Persia speech.

'Sit down here please,' he said when we were in his home. 'Have you plenty of· cushion on your very good self, or would you like another one?'

Just then, the electricity failed.

'God is great help, you see. He is very kind and turn off the light. He remind me to pray.' And unrolling his prayer mat, he began his invocations in a corner of the room, undisturbed by Hasan-'Ali's and my continued conversation. When he had finished, he looked round and said:

'Do you think me rude having my bottom to you while I prayed? But how can I apologise? I was facing God and that is better, isn't it, sir? An Englishman once told me it was rude to move my bottom up and down in front of him. Why was it rude? I made no noises with my bottom. Did he think it was too fat? But I tell you, sir, his was fatter. And it was good exercise. Mohammad was clever, making us move at least three times a day.'

Any advantage of such exercise was soon counteracted by the dinner—rice cooked with nuts, sultanas and saffron, bowls of curried meat, pickles, sugared plums and yoghourt. I found it a welcome change from the largely unspiced food of the Iranians.

Jesus Christ had gone to Tehran for two days, and when I suggested to Hasan-'Ali that we go and see if he was back, he put the matter to God and his beads. No, he said, Jesus Christ would not be back yet. But my belief was less firm, and we agreed to go and see. We reached Jesus' house and knocked on the door, but there was no reply.

'It is the Will of God,' said Hasan-'Ali, quietly and without triumph.

As we walked back along the street, a robed figure hurried towards us and raised a hand in greeting. God must have changed his mind, for it was Jesus Christ.

'Come and have some food,' he said, without surprise. Perhaps God had warned him too.

Though he was tired, he prepared a meal, and we settled against the walls to talk.

'Now how far have we got?' he asked.

'I was learning that Jesus has a sense of humour,' I said. 'So will you tell me what Islam thinks of Christ?'

'Yes, of course, for Islam loves Christ—but as a person, God's messenger, not God Himself. Remember, though,

> 'It is not fruitful to tear down men's
> beliefs, if goodness comes from them—
> and Christians teach love, though
>   their reason is lacking.
> For consider, what is one plus one plus one?
> Three you will say, yet they say one,
> That Jesus is the Father is the Spirit.
> Yet Jesus was a mortal, with mortal needs
>   of water, food and clothing.
> How can that be? For God is God, His
> needs are none, all stand
>   in need of Him.
> *So believe in God and His Messengers,*
> *and say not "Three". Refrain: better is it*
> *for you. God is only One God. Glory be*
> *to Him—that He should have a son!*
> *To Him belongs all that is in the heavens*
> *and in the earth; God suffices*
>   *for a guardian.**

'And if God is the begetter of Jesus, then why should Jesus be divine? Adam was created by God, but no-one calls him the Son of God. If Jesus is God, and if He died and descended into hell, then where was God in this world for those three days?'

I thought about this, and nearly rejected it as a simplistic view. But I realised that this was the Muslim way of teaching, so that even

* Quran, 4 'Women'.

the unsophisticated could understand. And the stories, taken from everyday life, made the most complex arguments understandable.

'The Hindus, they have difficulty with their trinity too,' said Hasan-'Ali. 'Sat, Cit and Ananda—Being, Consciousness, and Joy. Some say their Being is in East Africa, their Consciousness in India, and their Joy in a bank in England.'

Jesus Christ nodded and continued the argument. 'We think of Jesus as a messenger of God who wrought miracles. Does God need to work miracles to prove Himself? We cannot understand how Christians have so misinterpreted his teachings. Perhaps it is just that they have no clear book for guidance—the gospels were chosen arbitrarily by the Council of Nicaea from many others written.'

'But surely the Muslims equally misunderstand the teachings of Mohammad? Look at the number of sects in Islam.'

'You've put your finger on the point,' said Jesus Christ. 'Islam. *Within* Islam. It is still one great community which over-rides the differences:

> 'Islam is a force, the unity of men
> who accept one God, the same great
> God, with Mohammad as His Messenger
> and the Book as His Word.
>
> 'Islam is a force which has spread across
> the world, through wisdom and light;
> There may be diversion, men may dispute,
> but no-one can deny
> the basic truths.

'To be a Muslim is the vital element, and then it's a matter for conciliation: the four Sunni sects recognise each other, and recently they recognised the Shi'as, so that any Sunni can perform his duties according to Shi'a belief.'

He detailed the present activities in the Muslim world for conciliation: Islamic World Congresses and Islamic conferences for all sects; a centre in Cairo where scholars from all branches study, and publish their findings; the Islamic Research Academy in Karachi which facilitates research on Islam, its ideology, history and culture. And all these organisations combine an academic approach with a practical one, presenting to Muslims a clear idea of the values by which they live.

'But aren't the Imams an insoluble problem? I mean, neither side will accept the other's Imams?'

'That is probably true, but as I've said before, the important thing is belief in God and right living. There's not much difference between sects on the practical side—laws covering daily life, commerce, charity, politics. They're all clearly set out in the Quran and there's little chance of misinterpretation. But when the day comes, the Sunnis will realise their error. They're like the grammarian who was crossing a river and thought he had knowledge.

' "Do you know any grammar?" he asked the boatman.

' "No, sir, I know little."

' "Then you have wasted half your life!"

'But a storm came and turned the boat over.

' "Do you know how to swim, sir?" cried the boatman.

'The grammarian was sinking rapidly, and cried out "No!"

' "Then you've wasted all your life," said the boatman, and swam to the bank.'

Jesus Christ added: 'Surely the Sunnis will know when the Hidden Imam returns according to the signs.

> 'And the signs for His appearance are many,
> So know you when He comes. For first will come
> the Dajjal, a one-eyed man who is skilled in magics.
>   Shouting will there be, in the sky,
>   like thunder: "The Righteousness is come."
> Then will a man of pure lineage be murdered
> in Mecca, and the sun shall eclipse the moon
> and the moon the sun, at the end of Ramadan.*

> 'Such signs are definite, but these are probable:
> Many earthquakes will there be, and killings
> in the world; the sky, the whole sky will be
> red, and the rain will pour down on the desert.
> In the East a star will come in the shape
> of a moon. And men will sin, and women even
>   will dress as men.'

* An Islamic month lasting thirty days. During this time, Muslims fast from sunrise to sunset.

'Ah yes, women,' I said casually. I had purposely avoided the subject until now. 'A bone of contention between Muslims and the West.'

'Yes, but unnecessarily so,' said Jesus Christ. 'For the teachings of Islam give them equal duties and equal rewards:

> '*And whosoever does deeds of righteousness,*
> *be it male or female, believing—*
> *they shall enter Paradise, and not be wronged*
> *a single date-spot.**
> And from a single soul God created men and
> women and scattered them abroad.
> *They are a vestment for you, and you*
> *are a vestment for them.*†

> 'Now a human brain has three cells:
> thought, emotion and wish.
> Of these, the woman has mainly
> emotion and wish.
> Certainly she has intellect,
> but her intuition is greater.
> For that we respect her, we honour her,
> and we accord her the hardest task
> of rearing children.

'By the way, John, did you know that if a woman's praying, a man can't interrupt her, though he may interrupt his brother? And he may never enter her room without her permission. In addition he must respect her body:

> '*They will question thee concerning*
> *the monthly course. Say: "It is hurt;*
> *so go apart from women during*
> *the monthly course."* '‡

I found it difficult to give my reactions. Should I as a boy be embarrassed by such details? And if I showed embarrassment, would it prove that I was not the worldly boy I made myself out

---

* Quran, 4 'Women'.   † Quran, 2 'The Cow'.
‡ Quran, 2 'The Cow'.

to be? It was too complicated, and I tried to be as natural as he was.

Though I felt at ease by now in the company of Jesus Christ and Hasan-'Ali, yet somehow I felt uncomfortable. Perhaps it was my deceit, for they had shown me openness and sincerity, friendship and humour, while I was purposely concealing from them something which went against their very beliefs. I wanted to stay in Qum, to participate further in this religious life, and to learn more about Islam. I felt I had touched only the surface, even though that surface seemed misleadingly smooth, misleadingly simple. So many of the rules, the recommendations, the beliefs of Shi'a Islam seemed clear and easy to grasp. Yet I felt that below there was something far more complex, more intricate, of philosophies and theological arguments which were beyond my understanding. Perhaps, if I could have more time here, I would manage to go deeper, to understand the mystical undertones of Islam, its esoterics, its thought patterns. Perhaps I would just understand, for I felt here in Qum that the religious leaders and teachers were closer to knowledge of truth than I had encountered in people elsewhere.

But I could not stay. I was betraying their trust in me, and in a way, I was betraying myself, in my constant suppression of feeling and response.

I looked at Jesus Christ. 'I shall have to leave soon,' I said sadly.

He nodded. 'Yes, you have many other things to do. We should never neglect our duties and our business—activity is blessed by God. Go and look John, and when you look, try to remember some of the things we have talked about.'

'And come back, won't you?' said Hasan-'Ali. 'Come and tell us what you have seen. God, and the effects of Islam, are everywhere, you know, not just in Qum.'

Isfahan, a City of Crafts

I DECIDED to take a circuitous route from Qum along the edge of the eastern deserts which stretch some five hundred miles to the Afghan border. Salt lakes, slime, loose stones and sand, monopolise that area, and I could sense the vast nothingness from the white aridity of the land we passed through. Though it was early morning, the heat in the overcrowded bus was stifling, and the women flapped their veils against their faces, and wiped the sweat from their panting children.

We drank warm water from plastic bottles, and sucked chips of ice stored in a small refrigerator beside the driver. The conductor began to collect a few *toman** from each person, for the ice and service I thought. But the bus stopped near a knoll, in which was a niche where a man was sitting. When the driver called out, he got up and limped towards us.

'Peace be with you,' said the driver.

'And in your kindness, peace to you and your company,' answered the beggar.

'How is it with you today?'

'There is silk round my body and roses in my hair.' His clothes and hair were straggled and grey from dust.

'What are your needs, old one?' asked the driver.

'What needs have I when there is sun for my light, and a grain of sand to contemplate? And even now I'm rewarded with the vision of your face.'

The driver laughed and held out the coins. The beggar took them hastily and placed them in his shirt.

'Blessings,' he said. 'Such coins will make a fine pattern on my floor.'

The bus moved on, and the driver turned to the man behind.

'That old man has been there for weeks. I'll bet he's got quite a pattern of empty bottles.'

We reached Kashan at noon to find deserted streets and doors

---

* Approximately 20 = £1.

closed against the heat, and I took the opportunity to wander round without a *cortége* of children. Once, this town had been prosperous, when it lay on the trade route of caravans which came with their burdens of spices. From the twelfth to fourteenth centuries it was a centre of pottery; in the sixteenth, it excelled in silk carpets. The Ardebil Carpet* is inscribed, 'The work of the slave of the threshold, Maqsud of Kashan, in the year 946 [A.D. 1531]'.

The carpet industry continues, rivalled now by Qum, but the town seemed lifeless, deprived of a position on modern trade routes. Even in the evening when it was cooler, there was little activity. In the back streets I saw a man wobbling between the open drains on his bicycle, and a few women hurrying home with bundles of food. All round, the blank walls muted the noises of family life.

When it was growing dark, I emerged from an alley into near emptiness. The land stretched flatly into the distance, its desolation increased by the repetition of squat bushes. A wind blew in, bringing dust and the contorted remnants of scrub, which slithered along the base of the walls. The walls conceded few openings, though behind, in the town, the first lights were quavering.

I chose a hotel which made no attempt at showiness. A fat man in a vest and baggy pyjama bottoms sat dozing behind a bowl of plastic flowers.

'Have you got a cheap bed on the roof?' I asked.

'We don't have a roof,' he grunted.

'How much are your rooms then?'

'We don't have a room.'

'A bed?'

'Fifteen *toman* a night. Double room.'

I turned to leave.

'All right then, twelve for you. But no less. We've got scorpions.'

Two youths were listening and said insistently:

'Please, come and share our room. There's a spare bed—you can have it free.'

I made the excuse that I was feeling ill, and asked for a separate room. But they followed me in. I lay on the bed groaning; they

* Acquired by the Victoria and Albert Museum on the advice of William Morris.

sat either side, watching, The smaller was wearing a pale blue suit, his hair sleeked back, his nails carefully manicured. He asked if he could bathe my head. The other was burly, and had large stains of sweat across his shirt. He scratched his nose as he talked, and kept wiping his hands on his thighs. Again they asked me to share their room.

'Don't worry about me,' I said. 'I'm sure you've plenty to do.'

'All our time is for you,' said the svelte one.

'We've finished our work,' said the other.

'What work do you do?' I asked.

'We're merchants,' said the first.

'Of silk carpets?'

'Of chewing gum and bubble gum,' said the second, and burst a pink bubble between his lips.

The hotelier came in with some forms, and to my dismay asked for my passport. Coming to the photograph, he looked up at me, then studied it in more detail, then looked up again.

'This is you?' he asked, with such surprise that the two men went to look. They talked rapidly among themselves, and then left the room, taking my passport with them. A few minutes later, the heavier youth returned and sat down on my bed. He stared at me.

'You have eyes like almonds,' he said with a sigh and a quick glance to see whether the door was properly closed.

'They're diseased,' I said. 'With nut-mould.'

'But your lips are like Spring.'

I drew back my lips. 'And my teeth are like Autumn.'

He took my hand. 'Marry me.'

'I'm already engaged.'

'Marry me, just for one night.' And he leant towards me.

'No,' I said, pushing him away. But he grabbed my arms.

'Don't,' I cried. But I suddenly thought if I yelled too loud, it would only bring more men in, men who knew my identity. I struggled, and then remembered Jesus Christ's words.

'Would you tarnish your sword with my blood?' I asked.

He looked surprised, and immediately let me go.

Late that night I crept onto the balcony which ran in front of my room, and in the dark, began washing myself and my clothes in a small basin I had noticed at one end. I heard a cough behind me, and looking round, I saw a man tip-toeing towards me. Did he think I was a thief, for no-one normally stirred at this hour? Or did he know I was a girl? He might even think me a homo-sexual.

Keeping my back to him, I whispered in a deep voice: 'Darling, my sweet life, what pearls you have.'

I sighed deeply, and the man scuttled back to his room.

The garden of Fin lies a few miles outside Kashan, surrounded by high walls, so that once inside, I could see only blue sky and craggy hill-tops, acting more as a backdrop for intimacy than a reminder of natural phenomena. In the centre stood a pavilion built for his pastime by Shah Abbas, the great Safavid monarch who restored Persia's stability and revived her art in the late sixteenth century. Its walls were a skeleton of arches, through which I could see each part of the garden—the geometrically shaped flower-beds, the trees, the watercourses.

I was surprised by the garden. Not that I was expecting it to be 'packed with colour, enchantingly pretty, endearingly senti-mental', as Miss Sackville-West imagines a typical English garden, for I knew Persian gardens to be more formal. They are often divided into a grid, once of cosmological significance but now more of tradition. But as I walked round, I could see only that the right-angled paths of Fin were dusty and hot, with scant shade from the poplars and cypress trees, and air unsweetened by the scent of flowers. Even the freshness of the pools was reduced by the slime on the turquoise tiles, and the watercourses reminded me of footbaths at a swimming centre.

My lack of understanding of the Persian garden was confirmed when later in Qum I was talking to Jesus Christ.

'So you didn't like Fin?' he had asked.

'Not really. It didn't seem much refuge from the desert.'

'Ah, but the thought of that water, those flowers. That is what's beautiful. They are the symbols of fertility, the very essence of life. The garden means that to the Persian. And more. A place for protection and privacy, a place for medi-tation.'

We sat looking at the floor. It was a garden carpet, with swirls and gushes of flowers, water and cypress trees.

'And much of the concept is linked with Paradise,' he continued. 'For in Islam, Paradise is a place of abundance, consisting of two Gardens:

> *'therein two fountains of running water—*
> *O which of your Lord's bounties will you and you deny?*
> *therein of every fruit two kinds—*
> *O which of your Lord's bounties will you and you deny?*
> *reclining upon couches lined with brocade,*
> *the fruits of the gardens nigh to gather—*
> *O which of your Lord's bounties will you and you deny?"**

And as he talked, so my memory of the garden became beautiful. Perhaps this, I thought, the fusion of fact and ideal, was the keynote of the Persians. Perhaps this explained the elaborateness of their language, their exaggeration in praise and description.

The next small town was Natanz, a place set some distance from the main road and concealed among trees and small hills. It had an air of neglect, for the central street was pitted, the *chai khane* deserted, and the houses unrepaired.

I went to visit the Mongol mosque and a nearby tomb whose pyramidal dome was patterned with brickwork. When it was nearly dark, I returned to the tea-house. A young man was stretched on a bench, and he turned his head to stare at me.

'Is there a hotel in Natanz?' I asked.

He continued to stare.

'Is there anywhere I can stay the night?'

He pointed lethargically above him. 'There's a floor up there. Five *toman*.'

'For the floor? I can sleep on the ground for nothing.'

He closed his eyes. 'The gendarmes are just up the road. They won't like you sleeping outside.'

It gave me an idea, and I walked to the gendarmerie. An officer questioned me, though to my relief he did not ask for my passport; he said I could stay the night, and showed me a bench in the

* Quran, 55 'The All-Merciful'.

courtyard, where I stretched myself out. I was falling asleep when a door in the wall opened and some gendarmes came in, their rifle-barrels bobbing in my direction. They were dressed in khaki uniform which was frayed at the cuffs, and their trousers were crudely patched. They clustered round inquisitively—muscular men, and agile, who kept moving about as though their limbs were made of rubber bands.

One of them brought a pair of weights, skittle-shaped but much larger. He stood them on the ground and took hold of the handles. With a sudden contortion of the face, he heaved them shoulder high, holding them there with quivering muscles. Then his body loosened and he let them thump to the ground. Someone else ran over and took off his shirt: his chest was hairless and narrow, signs of a recent conscript. He clutched the handles and jerked. Nothing happened. He tried again. The onlookers laughed. An older man walked over and effortlessly lifted the clubs above his head with outstretched arms. Then he began to swing them in arcs about his body.

A man fetched a tin washing-bowl, holding it sideways between his legs, and beating with his fingers and the front of his wrist. His neighbour chanted in a cracked voice; the gymnast continued his movements like a miming dancer. Then he lay on the ground, face down, and raised himself with his arms. The spectators counted and clapped in time: forty, thirty, down to one. At each number, the man swooped to the ground and levered himself up in a circular motion. The counting worked upwards, growing faster. The body kept in time. Forty-nine, fifty. The body stopped, motionless.

I was seeing the national sport of Iran, which originated as training for resistance movements after the Arab invasion: the equipment used is still aggressive with clubs and shields, and a weapon resembling a bow.

The gymnast bowed and came up to me.

'Please, why don't you try your skill?' he said, pointing to the clubs.

'I mustn't lift heavy things,' I stammered, apprehensively. I looked up a word in my dictionary. 'I've had tuberculosis.'

'Weren't you in the army then?' he asked.

'No, they wouldn't have me.'

The men agreed I must be weak, and some moved away to play cards.

'Won't you dance then?' asked the gymnast. And the others began to sing and clap.

I could think of no excuse, so merely shook my head. Somebody else got up to dance: he slid between us with lithe arm movements and sensual twists of the body. He jumped and shuddered, and finally embraced the trunk of a tree.

We went to bed, and I was given a bunk. But I slept little, for, throughout the night, gendarmes stamped in and out, clutching their bayonets, smoking and talking. A few came to peer at me, sometimes touching my shoulder or face, but I lay motionless, pretending to be asleep. Fortunately none pursued it, though one man caressed my cheeks for some minutes.

From Qum, the city of Isfahan seemed a natural progression, a transition from theory and reflection to practice and organic expression, where the effects of doctrines and disciplines are seen in buildings, in decoration, in craftsmanship. The perfection of a petal in mosaic faience, the elegance of script spelling praise to God, even the shape of a courtyard: all give some indication of the meaning of Islam.

It was Isfahan as a centre of crafts that I particularly wanted to study, to see the relationship of the work with Islam, and at the same time to find techniques and designs which I could use in England. I booked into a hotel which gave me a room on the roof, a salmon pink room with a mauve carpet and yellow bedspread. Huge cauldrons sat near my window, filled with fermenting tomatoes and chillis, and a woman ironed sheets on the hard mud floor.

I spent the first day cleaning myself and my clothes, for I had the luxury of a shower and hot water. I washed and cut my hair and nails, and for the first time I was able to wash my chest-girdle, for I sat in my room quite safely while it dried in the sun outside.

The next day I went to the bazaar where many of the craftsmen worked, either in backrooms or their own small shops. I saw copper vessels beaten out and welded; silver bowls embossed with a hammer and nails; brass lamps pierced with intricate patterns; tin buckets made from old petrol cans. Women knotted carpets while men heaved wool through vats of dye; and men also printed, by hand, lengths of cotton and silk. Their right hands were protected with a wadge of rubber and rags, and they slammed down rhythmically on the wooden blocks.

I sat for a long time watching the printers work, and they let me take impressions on paper of their blocks. The patterns were mainly traditional, Safavid style—undulating vines, stylised flowers, wide-eyed birds and the paisley seed-pod. But some showed outside influences: a giraffe, an aeroplane, an Aztec-type pattern.

The block-maker was in a small room up narrow and steep stairs. He was digging with a knife on a piece of planed pearwood while his assistant glued patterns on his next assignment. I commissioned some blocks of my own design which were based on traditional Persian patterns—I wanted to use them for printing on suede in England. When I went to collect them, one had a jagged scar across it, so the cutter agreed to reduce the price. Then he pulled out some papers from under his bench; they were animated sketches of huntsmen, four of which I selected.

'That's forty *toman*,' he said.

'Oh come, they're very crumpled at the edges.'

'They're old. Very rare.'

'Four years old? I'll give you fifteen *toman*.'

'Do you want to rob me? I'll give them away for twenty-five.'

'You must think I'm rich. Eighteen.'

'Nineteen.'

'Oh all right, a pound.' I handed over seven pounds, the sum we had originally agreed for the blocks.

On another day, I arranged through Michael Halstead, the head of the British Council, for a meeting at the Department of Economics, to discuss the possibility of samples for export. I felt that as I might later be dealing with them from London as a girl, I should dress accordingly, and I went to the bazaar to buy some clothes. Several people looked at me curiously as I tried on a pair of women's shoes beneath my baggy trousers; and rather than suffer further embarrassment, I chose a large cotton dress without trying it on. I did not dare buy a bra, so I bought some sellotape instead. The next morning I walked to the Department feeling uncomfortable and strangely vulnerable with my legs and arms bare. Michael was waiting outside and we walked up the stone steps, to be shown into a huge room. An intricate carpet swept across to a leather-topped desk which was bare except for some telephones and a miniature flag of Iran.

We sat in armchairs, waiting for the man behind the desk to finish his telephone conversation. He was pale-faced, with puffy cheeks, and his body was squashed into a cotton suit. Finally he turned to us, greeting Michael and nodding to me. And though I asked all the questions, he addressed the answers to Michael. I asked about export regulations, and he gave a full explanation, but in child's language, as though I were incapable of understanding anything else. I began to feel resentful. If I had been in my boy's clothes, I felt sure he would have talked directly to me, and rated my abilities higher.

Afterwards I was shown the work of those craftsmen whom the Department represented. We visited silversmiths, cloth-printers, jewellers and enamellers; we saw mirror frames painted in lacquer, and wooden boxes inlaid with tiny mosaic. And I noticed a difference in the craftsmen's attitude now that I was dressed as a girl. Each produced his most fanciful, and often gaudiest work: trinkets, rings, small boxes, mirrors. And when I asked questions about discounts, technique and materials, they were surprised and often amused.

By the end of the day, we had watched multifarious processes and examined hundreds of articles, yet I did not feel satiated. Rather the more I looked at one thing, the more I understood the next. For there is a recurrence of theme, a repetition of pattern throughout Persian art, whether on silver cigarette boxes, tile mosaic, or brass pots. Full-blown flowers spring from twining stems, geometrics interlock, people sit in gardens, and always Quranic script flows along borders, or mingles with the pattern. I did not find such repetition monotonous, so infinite were the variations and so intricate. To trace a line as it wound across and back was hypnotic, and increasingly peaceful.

These patterns, then, were part of a religious art, the expression of a faith I had learned about in Qum; but did they reflect the same qualities, the same feeling? There was a certain precision of pattern, a clarity which belied its complexity, and at the same time a softness of line which brought harmony, and an intricacy which

77

invited further study. Yet, as I looked at the work, I felt the delicacy and vigour which once had typified this Persian Islamic art were diminished. Often petals were coarse, colours harsh, and patterns stilted. Many of the carpets were knotted with thick wool so that the lines of the design were blurred; the glaze on pottery was often streaked; arabesques on a silver bowl sometimes bumped against each other. Perhaps it was the effect of tourism; perhaps also that in being retrospective, the craftsmen were growing stale. But probably increased agnosticism was destroying the very meaning of the art, so that there was not the same devotion, the same articulation, to express a man's beliefs in the most perfect way.

I arranged with Mr. Hatamzaadi at the Department to have some buckles made of various metals and styles. When I went for a meeting, he had just returned from Shiraz.

'Ah, the roses,' he said, 'and the nightingales of Shiraz.' He leant over his desk to smell a crimson rose propped in a plastic cup. He took it out and gave it to me.

'Please, take this. What can be sweeter than roses?—except of course sweet women.'

Three craftsmen came into the room and studied my sketches. One was dressed in a dark grey suit and his hair was carefully greased into waves. He raised an eyebrow at one of the patterns.

'We've never done anything like this before,' he said. 'I don't know if my men can do it. And silver? It'll cost at least sixty *toman*, and we'll need several weeks to do it.'

'I'm afraid that's too expensive,' I said. 'We'd never be able to sell them.'

He shrugged, and handed the sketch to the next man. He was a small man, with bent shoulders and a thick neck from which protruded purple veins.

'What is it anyway?' he asked, turning the paper in every direction.

'A buckle.'

'Do you want us to make the belt too?'

'No, just the buckle.'

'Well we'd like to make the belt. The two of them, they'd cost . . . ' He counted on his fingers. 'Thirty-five *toman*.'

The third man wore a dirty cloth apron over his sweat-stained shirt. His hands were dry and cracked, and his right thumb-nail was black from a bruise.

'Silver? Could we plate it? That'd make it cheaper. And this relief work. Do you want this pattern exactly, or can we use some of our own?'

'Both, I should think.'

'And this edge. It looks a bit sharp. We'd better round it a bit more.'

He pulled out a rule from his apron pocket and measured the width of the buckle. 'It'll cost six *toman*. I'm afraid I'll need a week to make them.'

I accepted his offer, and a few days later went to his workshop to see how the buckles were progressing. It was a dark room lit by a dim electric bulb. Shavings of metal and lumps of tar were lying on the floor, and a wooden stool acted as his tool bench. He cleared the hammer and nails away, and asked me to sit down, ordering the young boy beside him to fetch us some tea. In his lap was a silver bowl, its body filled with tar, its surface marked out with a pattern. He picked up his hammer, chose a nail, and placing the point on a line of the pattern, tapped several times until the nail was indented to the right level. He continued to tap, moving the nail fractionally every second along the line. He stopped, and picked up another nail, more coarse, and tapped out a petal, twisting the nail in several directions.

'What does the pattern mean?' I asked.

He looked up and stared at me. 'Mean? It's a pattern.'

'But does it have any significance?'

'Why should it?' He held the bowl up. 'Is it good?'

'Yes.'

'Then isn't that enough?'

'Yes.'

'This pattern,' he said, running his finger along the lines. 'It's got flowers, and leaves. They're beautiful things. And this animal. It's a lion. A lion has strength you know.'

'And you don't mind repeating the same patterns?'

'Why should I? It's my work, I was brought up to do it. I'm lucky to be able to do it. And I do it as best I can.'

He began tapping again, his hand moving the nail along with complete steadiness, his eyes never leaving the line he was following. He finished an arabesque; then standing up, he ran his hand along a shelf above his head. It felt its way under some crumpled papers, and stopped, taking hold of something. The man pulled out some buckles, and gave them to me.

'Here, I've done these for you.'

They were perfectly proportioned, their surface slightly curved to fit the waist, their edges smooth and rounded. On the top swirled a pattern, similar to that he had just been making, but in miniature. Little flowers were dotted between curling leaves, framing a bounding lion.

'And these,' he said, pulling out some more. 'I hope you don't mind, I made some different shapes.'

One was square, another star-shaped and punctured with circular holes. But across each one, a delicate pattern grazed the metal.

'You've done a wonderful job,' I said with delight.

'God's mercy is always great,' he said, with a slight bow.

Still dressed as a girl, I walked along to the shop of a miniaturist to meet a mutual friend, but as he had not come, I watched the painter work. He sat motionless, cross-legged on a bench, his white hair trimmed to half an inch. His right hand filled in a disc of ivory with tiny strokes. Ant-sized horsemen galloped across a plain, tilting their pin-like spears towards the enemy; bodies on the ground spurted blood, and behind, tents and people peered out from jagged rocks and streams. His son was painting its mount, with thousands of blue dots. He kept measuring the margins with the frame, a wide one in red and gold marquetry.

Then the miniaturist picked up some white paper. He dipped his brush in black paint and outlined a face looking upwards. He added a turban, a beard and a moustache.

'This is Hafiz,' he said. 'Our poet, looking to Heaven for inspiration.'

'It's very fine,' I replied.

'Please, then, keep it.'

'No, I couldn't do that.'

'But you must, as I am your servant.'

Abbas arrived, a tall boy, half-Arab, half-Iranian, with sharp cheekbones and long fingernails. He spoke fluent English and had interpreted for me with some of the craftsmen. The painter asked us to lunch at his home, so the shop was locked, the blind drawn down, and we set off through the busy main street. We came to a quieter area where the streets had no shops, and stopped at a door in the high wall. It was opened by the painter's son, who took us through the garden into a white-washed room, where the food was laid out. The meal was large, though the painter apologised for its paucity. Then he produced a pack of cards and played poker with Abbas. As they slapped down the cards, they exclaimed with disgust or delight at the other's luck.

'Ace high,' said Abbas.

'A mouse's bite,' said the painter. 'I have a heifer here.' And he laid down a pair of tens. 'Did you know about the farmer?' he asked. 'He got kicked by a calf. So he started beating the poor old cow. Now why should he do that? "Well," said the farmer, "the calf was born innocent wasn't it? So where did it learn to kick? Only from its mother, so she must get the punishment."'

The painter dealt the next hand, and chuckled at his cards. After some bluff, he showed a single king.

'Sparrows!' cried Abbas. 'I've got a king and an ace. It's gold.' He shuffled the cards. 'An old man once found a pile of gold in the forest, but he didn't know what to do. For if he told the world, sure as sure they'd demand it from him. He didn't know if he could even trust his wife to keep the secret. So he said to her the next morning: "Wife, I've got a terrible secret. Don't tell anyone, but when I went to the lavatory, a sparrow flew out of my bottom." His wife promised to keep it to herself, but when she went to the well, she whispered to the butcher's wife: "It's a secret, but do you know, a *sparrow* flew out of my husband's bottom."

'So the butcher's wife told the butcher, and the butcher told the baker, and at the end of the day, when the shepherd met the old man, he said: "I've just heard forty sparrows flew out of your bottom. Wasn't it terribly painful?"

'Now what was the old man to do, if he couldn't tell his wife or anyone about the gold? Well, each night he left his house, and scattered some gold on the ground near some of his neighbours' doors. When they found it, they took it of course to the bank, explaining, "It was just lying in the street." And as more and more people banked small amounts of money, so the old man banked a small amount each day, saying: "It's just like everyone else. There seems to be gold in the streets." '

The painter had been losing gradually, and suddenly he took hold of my arm.

'Let me touch a dark-eyed woman for luck.'

'Don't let him,' said Abbas in English. 'Otherwise he'll think you're a prostitute. Just a flutter of eyelids, or a delicate play of the lips—anything like that shows you're a prostitute.'

I was so unused to female etiquette that I did not know what to do. Should I rudely shake off my host's hand? Or ask for something to cover my bare arms? But the painter released me and suggested I lie down in the next room for the afternoon.

'You mustn't tire yourself,' he said. 'I know how this heat affects my wife.'

'No, I'm fine,' I answered.

But he insisted and, as a girl, I felt I could not argue. The room had three large carpets, a low table laden with sweets and fruit, and a colour photograph of his sons in a silver frame. Round the walls hung several miniatures, almost identical to those I had seen in his shop. On a stool were six sketches, each one of Hafiz looking to Heaven, and each one the same as mine.

When I left the painter's house, I walked to the bazaar to buy some pottery bowls and for a distance of twenty yards I counted the number of functional items which were decorated. The pavement was patterned, the lamp-post, a door, a bucket holding walnuts. A water-carrier clinked ornamental cups which he filled from a worked brass container. There was a blind man's stick, a pair of dark glasses, and some scales outside a fruit shop.

In another shop, a man was squatting on the floor, surrounded by square tiles of different colours. A pattern was marked on their backs, and he chipped round the lines with a hammer. Then he fitted the pieces together, face down. Flowers and tendrils appeared, curving through a background of scroll-work and leaves.

'How do you keep the mosaic in place?' I asked.

The man looked up. One of his eyes was only a socket.

'We pour plaster on the back.'

'And is it for a mosque?'

'No, a garage.'

I noticed some pieces of glazed script in a corner.

'Are these for a garage too?'

'No, a mosque. It's from the Quran.'

Calligraphy has been and still is a vital part of Islamic art, an expression of beauty made holy because of its association with the Quran. Indeed a Quranic verse emphasises the divine qualities of writing:

> *Recite: And thy Lord is the Most Generous,*
> *who taught by the Pen,*
> *taught Man that he knew not.* *

For centuries, men have sought religious merit through calligraphy. One Ghaznavid Sultan copied out the Quran himself each year and sent it to Meshed;† the Mughal emperor Babur sent a copy to Mecca, written in a script he had devised specially for it.

Indeed the scripts themselves can convey an almost mystical emotion: spiky letters stabbing upwards, curved lines twining into arabesques, banded or crossed by thick bulbous script and interwoven with flowers and leaves. One royal patron said of a famous calligrapher in the sixteenth century:

> His handwriting is heart-ravishing like the down of beauties,
> It robs the heart of peace and the soul of patience,
> His pen is the wayward wizard
> Who throws the tresses of the night over the face of the day.‡

Even when the Mongols used printing in Persia for paper money, the Muslims refused to take advantage of the method. The Quran had been given in written form, and so must all books be. Indeed, the Quran was not printed in the Islamic world until the nineteenth century, and even then it was lithographed, as a less heretical method. And it was only early in the twentieth century that Egypt printed the Quran by letterpress.

---

* Quran, 96 'The Blood-Clot'. This *sura* (chapter) is meant to be the first revealed by Mohammad.

† Iran's holiest city where the Eighth Imam, Reza, is buried. The shrines of all the other Shi'a Imams are in Arabia and Iraq.

‡ Qadi Ahmad, *Calligraphers and Painters*, trs. V. Minorsky, Washington 1959.

It was hot and often frustrating work attempting to study the crafts, for the men were frequently absent, visiting either relatives or a holy shrine; or else they were praying, or eating, or sleeping in the heat of the afternoon. I was therefore glad for the break when some Iranians I had met in the bazaar offered to take me hunting. I was glad also that they knew me as a boy, for I was beginning to tire of the discrimination I had experienced as a woman.

We met one evening for dinner to discuss the plans for our expedition. Mohammad was twenty, sleekly dressed in green trousers and a white silk shirt. His cousin's hair stuck out, and Mohammad kept stroking it flat. Husain let him do it, and then shook his head to loosen his hair again.

The hunter wore a red plaid shirt, unbuttoned to show his white vest; his loose trousers were held up with a cord of leather, and his boots were studded with nails. His face was brown and deeply lined, and his body was lean, long-limbed.

'We call him *fateh*, the conqueror,' said Husain, gnawing a chicken bone.

'Not of men, though,' sighed Mohammad, sipping his coca-cola.

'How often do you go hunting?' I asked Fateh.

'Not so often, now. Licences are hard to come by, and the game's disappearing. I should think about ten days a month.'

'How much did you go before?'

'Weeks at a time. I walked everywhere, sleeping out, eating what I killed, carrying skins on my back. There was plenty of game then. Gazelle, leopard, ibex, quail. And prices were good. I lived like a rich man when I came to the towns.'

The tradition of hunting has been with the Persians for hundreds of years. Herodotus in the fifth century, B.C., said the Persians taught their sons three things: to ride horseback, use the bow, and speak the truth. But it reached its zenith with the Sassanians,* when excursions were treated as state ceremonies, lasting for a month or more. The king, with hundreds of attendants, hawks, horses, cheetahs, and heavily embroidered tents, would set off to slaughter animals and to feast. And one of their kings, Bahram Gur, is the Persian hunting hero. He killed lions on foot

* The Sassanian dynasty ruled for four hundred years until the Arab invasion in the mid-seventh century A.D.

with a sword; cut bucks in two, and lodged an arrow so deeply in a wild ass that neither the point nor shaft showed. He even 'sewed up with steel-points a dragon's mouth, whose venom scorched the brambles'.*

Many of his feats were depicted on magnificent silver plates, and still today some of the hunting scenes appear on Persian carpets in typical Sassanian style, to show that not only Islam is a strong influence in Persian art, but the sense of heroes and history as well.

When we had finished our meal, Mohammad suggested we stay at his house, and he laid out my bedding next to his. When the others were asleep, he put out an arm and touched me.

'John,' he whispered.

I began to snore gently.

'John,' he said, shaking me. 'John.'

I muttered and cursed as though in a nightmare, and tossed about until I was out of his reach.

The next morning, Mohammad murmured that he could not be bothered to come, so collecting food, knives, and water, the three of us set off in a rusty jeep.

We took the road to Najafabad, west of Isfahan, passing a few labourers walking to work in the dark. After forty minutes, we branched off the main road onto a dirt track and came to a village enclosed by walls. The sky was beginning to lighten, but there were no signs of movement, only a dog which scavenged outside. Fateh blew the horn, lengthily. A few minutes later he blew it again. A door opened in the wall and two men stumbled out, dragging on tattered jackets, their eyes still tight from sleep. Their bodies and faces were emaciated, and thick stubble darkened their chins. Each carried a felt hat, blackened with grease and the smoke of open fires.

'Peace,' said the two men, approaching the jeep.

'You seem to have had an excess of peace, in sleep,' said Fateh.

'So God would have it. Now we are prepared for hard work,' replied one of them as he settled himself in the back of the jeep and began to fall asleep. But sleep was impossible as we jolted along a track towards some foothills. The track swerved to the left, but we continued upwards, weaving between boulders and spiky

* *The Shahnámá of Firdausi*, Vol. VII, trs. A. G. & E. Warner, London 1915.

bushes until we stopped on the brow of a knoll. We got out and scanned the hill-faces.

'Look all round you,' Fateh said, 'for the game's moving up to hide in the hills.'

I had difficulty in adjusting my eyes to look for small specks in a large landscape: I did not know where to look in detail, nor which gulleys or paths the animals would take. The half-light did. not help, nor the blurred binoculars which Fateh lent me. We climbed back into the jeep and switch-backed over the foothills, frequently stopping as one of us pointed excitedly to an object, only to realise it was a boulder.

Dawn is not a lingering affair in Iran, despite its false starts. The sun rises quickly from behind the hills, so that deep shadows rapidly withdraw their protection to leave the ground increasingly hot.

'Well, that was no good,' said Fateh. 'We'd better try the tops.' And he turned the jeep up a steep slope. We traversed dry stream beds, gulleys, sand and stones, until we came to a plateau overlooked by rocky peaks. It was scattered with trees and boulders. The two labourers were set down near the highest peak, and we continued to an open-ended valley. Fateh stopped the engine, and pulled out the rifle; we hid ourselves in a square construction of low stone walls. To our left, the valley dropped to the plain several hundred feet below; in front of us a barren slope rose to the high peak we had passed in the jeep.

We sat down to wait, the rifle propped against the wall. I was beginning to grow drowsy in the heat when we heard a high-pitched call which echoed against the hills. A shrill whistle followed. I sat up and strained to look for movement on the hill-face. The other two continued to smoke a cigarette. I was surprised at their languor. Then I understood. A herd of animals appeared in the distance—no-one could miss them for they kicked up a screen of dust as they galloped down.

'Wild sheep,' muttered Fateh, and rolling himself over, took hold of the rifle and positioned himself against a wall. The sheep drew nearer, spurred on by the yells of the beaters. They crossed the valley in which we lay, some two hundred yards below us. They stopped for a moment to look round. The rifle cracked. One of the sheep jumped, as though on a tight metal spring. The herd galloped away, their heads seemingly weighed down by thick horns which curved round their shoulders.

'I think you must have hit it,' I said with concern.

Fateh shook his head. 'It was a clean miss.' He looked at me reprovingly. 'You didn't offer me God's blessings in my aim.'

I apologised and we got up and walked to the spot. We could find nothing, but before giving up, I examined once more the place I had marked. This time I found it.

'Blood. Here.' I pointed down. Fateh hurried over.

'Yes. Very good . . . John.' He seemed annoyed that a boy should rival his skills.

Then began the exertion, as we trailed the blood spoor like Red Indians. It was now midday, when the sun was at its hottest and the reflection from the stones made it hotter. We climbed over boulders and shingle, we balanced precariously on minute tracks, each taking it in turn to point dramatically and exclaim 'Blood here'. But gradually the splashes grew smaller until we were searching the ground fruitlessly.

Fateh gave instructions. 'Husain, you go back and bring the jeep round to the flats beneath us. John, you climb down there.' He pointed to a precipice. 'See if the animal has fallen over, then meet up with the jeep. Both of you drive along and scan this face. We three will continue along here.'

I began scrambling down the steep face. The ground was crumbly, so I clutched the prickly bushes. They too became dislodged. I stopped to steady myself. The plain below stretched into a line of ice-coloured mirage before rising to another range of mountains. The stillness was absolute. There was no-one to be afraid of: only a fool, I thought, would be here. But I was afraid, afraid of falling, down onto sharp rocks to land in some crevice where the vultures would find my body to pick at.

I reached the bottom as the jeep came into sight. We bumped along at the foot of the hills, and after a mile, stopped. We waited for twenty minutes and then saw the three men clambering down towards us. As they approached, we called to each other: 'No good. Saw nothing', so Husain and I unloaded the lunch.

We sat in silence, chewing stale bread and slices of warm meat. We washed out our mouths with water, then Fateh positioned himself with his rifle.

'You see that small white stone there?' He explained its position about three hundred yards away. He adjusted his sights and squeezed the trigger. A line of dust flew up six inches to the right of it. He breached the rifle and fired again. This time he hit it.

An hour later, Fateh, Husain and I were piling stones in a ravine, to act as a hide-out. I picked up one and disturbed a scorpion. It scuttled beneath another. Then we sat down and waited once more.

Fateh looked up at the caves which studded the sides of the ravine.

'I killed a leopard here last year.'

I looked respectful.

'Oh, that's nothing. Some years ago, I was caught in a snow-storm. I spent four days trudging through the mountains. I had to kill six wolves. Then I ran out of bullets—I killed two more with my knife.'

This time four gazelle sped past us, and though I gave the appropriate blessing, Fateh would not shoot while they were running.

We drove home in the late afternoon, passing women who were filling sacks with herbs, and stopping by a pool which was fed by a *qanat*. It was surrounded by willow trees and we lay in the shade on some grass. One of the men lit a fire and boiled a kettle for tea, and as we sipped the hot liquid, a man came to unplug the pond; the murky water gushed into watercourses and sped down to the orchard and allotments below.

We left the two labourers at their village, and soon regained the main road. It was growing dark when we had a puncture, but we changed it quickly. It was dark when we had another puncture and we waited two hours while Husain took the wheel to be mended. We had a third puncture, and reached Isfahan at midnight. I thanked Fateh and Husain.

'The honour was ours,' replied Fateh. 'You make a good hunter.' He paused. 'Shall we make a partnership?'

I was flattered.

'That would be good,' I said. 'But I couldn't kill wolves, you know.'

'No. But you could carry the rifle.'

Isfahan, a City of Crafts

For me, Isfahan as a memory, an image, meant more than reality with its present-day jostle of hotels and factories. Its suburbs and new buildings have swept away the approaching vista of domes and its greenness and shade scarcely remain. Once the Chehar Bagh was a broad walk of pools and gardens, but now it is a paved promenade enclosed by a dual carriageway and lined with skimpy trees.

The monuments are still there, but many of them gleam with the newness of restoration and reminded me more of the Veneerings than Safavid grandeur. And I thought it sad that some of the mosques were frequented more by tourists than believers.

Whatever my misgivings, I found the tilework in the Safavid mosques resplendent—acres of it swimming with colour and pattern, stretching over arches, round pillars, under domes, now mosaic, now *haft rangi*,* mingling with unglazed brick and alabaster. And many of the themes I had seen elsewhere were repeated in the patterns: the undulating vines, the lotus flowers, the medallions and geometrics. But the colours were more vivid, glistening with blues, bright yellows and white.

After such profusion, I found the Friday Mosque a welcome change, for though there is Safavid tilework in the courtyard, its main body is unembellished brickwork, dating back to the eleventh century. Yet such brickwork provided its own patterns, and accentuated the shape of the structure. Lines of amber-coloured bricks circled into an upturned whirlpool or zigzagged into a star; they knitted themselves like a spider's web, across a vaulted chamber, and worked their way over walls like a blank wool tapestry.

It was pure form, but I did not find it overpowering, for there was delicacy and harmony, and a sense of movement from the bricks themselves and the many domes and arches. It seemed to have strength also, and I felt that the Persians had taken the vigour of their conquerors, the Seljuqs and Mongols, and injected it with their own sensitivity.

I sat down against a pillar to sketch some of the patterns, but with the heat of the afternoon, I fell asleep.

'Hey, wake up,' said a voice, and somebody tugged my hair, pulling my head up. 'You can't sleep here. It's a holy mosque.'

* Literally 'seven colours', the name given to square glazed tiles.

89

I looked up sleepily and saw a boy standing òver me, glowering.

'I've seen people sleeping in mosques,' I said irritably.

'Well, *you* can't. Come on, get up.' And he pulled my arm.

'All right, all right, I'm coming,' I said, and walked towards the main door. The boy must have regretted his brusqueness, for he ran after me.

'Mister, mister, do you want some melon?'

'No thanks'.

'But it's good melon. Please, you must come.'

We went into a small room nearby where an old man was sitting, his blue eyes squinting, his lower lip drooping. He looked up at us questioningly, but when the boy said 'Melon', he grinned. As he bit into a piece, the juice trickled down his chin and dropped onto his lap, but he merely rubbed it in.

The boy patted his knee and said:

'Tell us a story then.' He turned to me. 'This old man knows most of Firdausi by heart. He can really get those heroes thundering.'

The old man bent his head for a moment, and then looked at me.

'Have you heard of Rustam, young man?'

I nodded, remembering Matthew Arnold's poem.

'Then I'll tell you one of his many feats. The time he went to rescue his king, who was captured and blinded by the White Div. Rustam, the great warrior, sped over the vast plains on his swift and faithful horse, killing lions, thirst, and a wicked witch. And though he reached his king, he still had to slay the White Div before they could safely leave.'

The old man began to recite in a loud voice, articulating his words and moving his unfocussed eyes up and down with the rhythm.

> 'Then radiant as the sun he went to seek
> That Div, and found him in a pit like Hell;
> He could not see the sorcerer for murk,
> So paused, his sword in hand, and rubbed his eyes,
> Till in the gloom he saw a Mountain
> That blotted all within.

> 'Now Rustam did not slay that wretched Div
> Asleep, but roused him with a leopard's roar.

He charged at Rustam as an avalanche of rock—
His head in iron helmet, his two hands
Hurling out a millstone.

'Enraged, brave Rustam struck the Div and cut
A hand and foot from that enormous bulk.
They wrestled, tearing out each other's flesh,
Till all the ground was soaked with both their blood.
And Rustam thought: "If I survive this day,
Then never shall I die."

'But still they wrestled, streaming blood and sweat,
Till mighty Rustam, given strength by God,
Reached out a hand and clutched the Div and dashed
Him to the ground, then stabbed his heart so deep
That all his spirit died.

'He plucked the liver out from that grim beast:
The carcase filled the cave, and all the world
Was like a sea of blood. And with that blood
He rode back to his King, and smeared it
On his eyes, and on the others' eyes,
So they could see again.'*

I had two more tasks to complete in Isfahan: to find a motorbike
and to investigate leathers. At home we were using Persian leather
—expensive, high quality skins—and I thought in Persia they
might be cheaper with greater variety of colour. I tried the shoe-
makers, but they showed me black and white leather only, and
scarlet plastic. In the alleyways beyond the bazaar, I found leather
bellows fanning small furnaces. The legs of a whole goatskin were
tied and the neck pulled round the blowpipe. Air was then
squeezed through the skin to the furnace.

I found saddlery and sheepskin jackets, but nothing else. Not
even a leather-bound book, for which the Persians were once so
famous, especially in the fifteenth century. Miniatures and calligraphy were enhanced by the elaboration of their binding—block
stamping and blind tooling, lacquer painting, relief embossing.

* Based on A. G. & E. Warner's translation, *The Shahnámá of Firdausi*, Vol. II,
London 1906.

Carlyle, an Armenian friend, said he could help and took me to his shoe-maker in the Armenian quarter. A tall man with stooping back and eyes which were red from strain got up as we entered the shop. He produced leathers and suedes in several colours, but they were scarred and unevenly dyed. It was only when I returned home that I learnt Persian leathers come from India—the name derives from the time they were brought through the Persian Gulf. But shagreen, an untanned leather patterned with circles, originated in Persia, as ass-skin. It was trampled with seeds when moist, and when dry, the seeds were shaken away to leave small indentations.

I also searched for a motorbike, for I felt I would see more of Iran that way, rather than travelling by bus. And certainly to reach the tribes in the south, I would need to walk or go by bike, for they were accessible only by mountain track.

I did not at first find a second-hand moped—I was frightened of handling anything heavier—and could not afford a new one. Again Carlyle offered to help, and after days of enquiries, he found one. The owner was a skinny man, with a bumpy, bony nose which seemed permanently to drip. He kept sniffing, grunting at the back of his throat as he did so; or else he blew out one nostril into the air while blocking the other with his finger.

I tried out the bike and was somewhat unnerved when the brakes did not work.

'How much?' said Carlyle when I finally returned.

'A very good price, sir,' said the man. 'Only thirty pounds.'

'Thirty pounds?' said Carlyle. 'That's ridiculous. Twenty-five pounds and the repair of the brakes.'

'But I paid twenty-nine,' simpered the man. 'And look what I've done.'

Plastic ribbons streamed from the handlebars, and fluorescent spikes wobbled at right angles to the wheels. But he finally accepted and agreed to repair it by the following day.

'And can you bring the registration book?' I called. 'I need it for insurance.'

The next morning the man did not come. We waited three days, and when we went to his workshop, he was there, but the bike was unrepaired.

'What could I do?' asked the man. 'My brother's ill, so how can

92

I work?' He raised his hands in despair. 'And only for twenty-five pounds.'

Carlyle grew angry. 'We'll take it now, without the repair. Just give us the registration book.'

'What? Oh yes.' He rummaged in a pile of dirty papers. 'I'm sorry. I don't seem to have it. You see the illness of my brother—'

'Have you ever had it?'

'Not exactly. I'm selling the bike for my brother.'

'Does he have it?'

'Well, no. *He* was given the bike by a man who owed him some money.'

'And that man doesn't have it, of course.'

The man looked pleased. 'You're right. So no-one knows where it is.'

'We'll hire the bike,' said Carlyle.

'But the price will drop after that.'

'Does the milometer work?'

'Not precisely.'

'Then we'll hire the bike.'

And we took it away, with its decorations. I bought a red plastic bottle for petrol, a white one for water, and a scarlet saddle-bag to sling on the back. Then I hazarded the traffic, following other cyclists for guidance. I went down one-way streets, the wrong way, I wove in and out of traffic, and with other motor-cyclists, I ignored the signals of policemen. And as an indication of its ways, I christened it Mephistopheles.

It was now my most manly accessory, but it also proved a vulnerable point, for what man in Iran owns a motorbike when he cannot even start it? I would pedal laboriously while the bike was propped on its stand and find either I had forgotten to turn on the petrol or that I had flooded the engine. Then a mocking group of boys would gather to tamper with the wires, destroying my confidence, until I was reduced to asking one of them to start it for me.

6 *Tribal Interlude*

THE SOUTH was to be a holiday, an exploration of the remote province of Fars, which gives its name to Persia and the language *farsi*, and whose history provides a galaxy of names in buildings and people: Persepolis, Cyrus, Alexander the Great, as well as Sassanians and Shirazi poets. My primary interest, however, was the Qashqai tribe who migrate across Fars each spring, and I hoped to study their designs. But it could be that I might not reach them, for they were bound in the mountains for the summer, and access was difficult without government passes.

I decided to take a bus to Shiraz, for I was told that not even champion motorbike riders used that stretch of road, so great was the risk of brigands.

The bus was leaving at seven in the morning, so I arrived early for my bike to be strapped to the roof. At half-past seven, the driver called:

'Come on, bring that motorbike here.'

I wheeled it over and stood helplessly wondering if I had to heave it up myself. The driver examined the petrol tank.

'But it's still full of petrol. It can't go like that. Empty it please.'

I turned Mephistopheles on his side, but only a trickle came out.

'Could you help?' I asked.

Cursing, the driver swung the bike over and I caught some of the flow in my petrol can. Then he yelled for a porter. An old man, his back bent permanently from the loads he had carried, came from behind the bus. Flinging a rope around it, he hoisted the bike on his back, and mounted the ladder at the side of the bus. Halfway up, he swayed with the weight, and I felt sure he was going to fall: I was ashamed I could do nothing to help. But he reached the top and tied it insecurely to the front.

The land we passed through was uncompromising in its bleakness and grandeur where the Zagros foothills swarmed to jagged peaks. Sunlight and paths prised themselves between outcrops of rock and then disappeared in the tiers of hills. The road sped

The main courtyard of the shrine at Qum

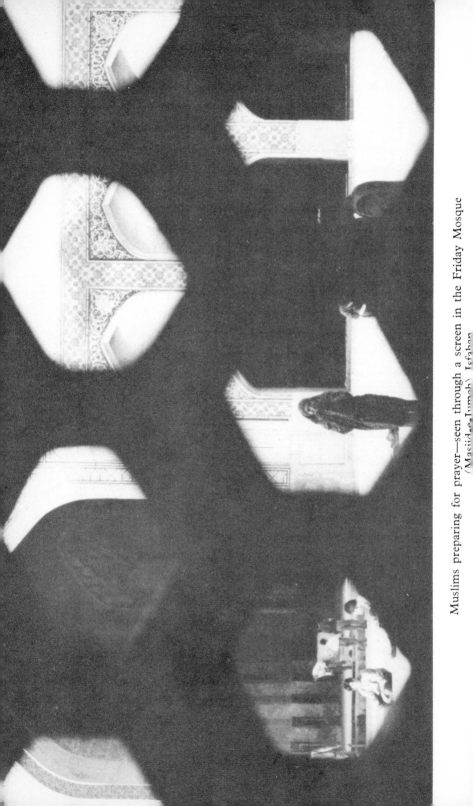

Muslims preparing for prayer—seen through a screen in the Friday Mosque (Masjid-e-Jumeh), Isfahan.

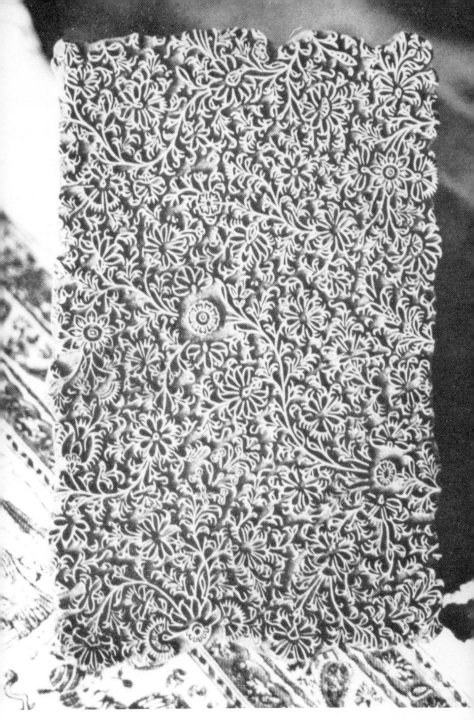

A wood-block, carved by hand, for printing on fabric

Tile mosaic in brilliant blues and yellows in the entrance to Madraseh Mader-e-Shah, Isfahan, built 1706–14

Craftsman printing a cotton mat, in the bazaar, Isfahan

Qashqai woman working on a tribal rug near Firuzabad

Qashqai women collecting water near Firuzabad

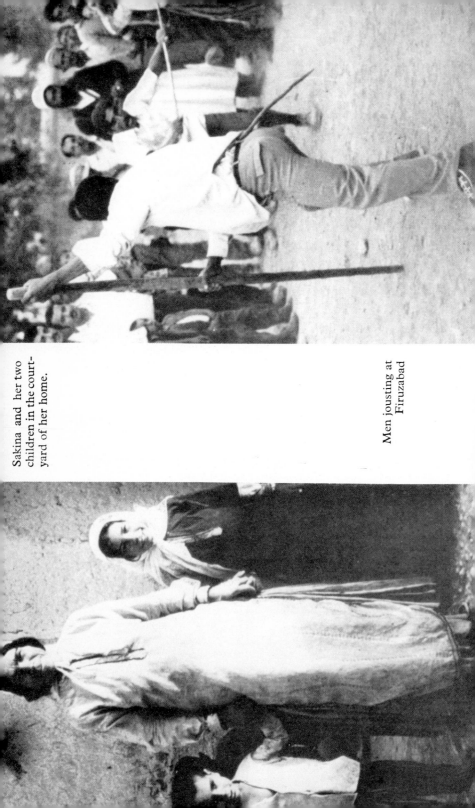

Sakina and her two children in the courtyard of her home.

Men jousting at Firuzabad

Antique Turkmen 'tiara', normally worn as a hat ornament. Made of silver, inset with cornelians, and damascened with gold

Turkmen tribesman, now sedentary. In the nineteenth century, the tribe lawlessly
controlled the area east of the Caspian Sea

Araf's mother spinning wool outside her home, near the fortress of Alamut

Araf's sister watching the carpet being weighed

Araf as guide in the mountains, where tracks were the only route. We were walking early in the morning from Alamut to Maymundiz through miles of scrubland and brown dust, passing small villages whose tea-houses competed for transient visitors. Towards evening, only silhouettes showed, defined against a whitening sky.

It was dark when we reached Shiraz and as soon as my moped was unloaded, I went to find a hotel. I felt uneasy without the protection of daylight to reconnoitre and to assess the mood of the town: at night, people seemed hostile, the buildings withdrawn, so I could not deduce what type of quarter it was. By chance, I found a Travellers' Rest House with cold running water and a bed in the garden by a non-flowering rose-tree. An electric bulb in the corner was too dim to read by, so I stretched out on my bed. Suddenly the shutters of a room upstairs banged open. A man and a woman leaned out. She was unveiled, and her white shirt stretched over ample breasts. She looked down, her greasy hair flopping against her red mouth. I smiled. Then the man looked down, and pushing the woman back into the room, he closed the shutters firmly.

Half an hour later, she came into the garden with a transistor and a plate of biscuits.

'You American?' she asked in broken yet twanging English.

'No, English.'

'You have money?'

'Not much.'

'You good?' She placed the biscuits and wireless on the bed, touching my thigh as she did so. 'You how old?'

'Twenty-three.'

She seemed puzzled.

'I'm no good,' I said. '*Khajeh,* eunuch.'

Immediately she let her breasts drop from their thrusting position and turned to go into the house.

'You've left your wireless and biscuits,' I called.

She shrugged. 'Use them.' And she tightened her body again as a man came out to meet her.

I turned on the wireless. Iranian music coiled the air; a mellifluous voice listed the number of children at school; a rhetorical voice announced:

'Good evening. This is the British Overseas Broadcasting Corporation. We are now relaying the fourth and final part of a dramatised version of *Wuthering Heights.*'

A wind ensemble transported me to nineteenth-century York-
shire. Catherine and Linton were ejected by Earnshaw and a voice
croaked:

'Aw were sur he'd sarve ye eht! He's a grand lad! He's gotten
t'raight sperrit in him! *He* knaws—aye, he knaws, as weel as Aw
do, who aud be t'maister yonder.—Ech, ech, ech! He mad ye
skift properly! Ech, ech, ech!'

A man of about thirty-three came and sat on my bed. I looked
up and he inclined his head.

'May God give you good health.'

I had to adjust myself quickly from the moors.

'To your kindness, I am well.'

'Do you understand?' he asked, pointing to the wireless. I
nodded and we sat listening, the man moving his hand like a
pendulum, his eyes closed. Some twenty minutes later the pro-
gramme ended, and I turned off the knob.

'That was good,' I said.

'Yes, very good,' said the man, though he had not understood a
word.

The following morning I saw little of Shiraz for I left for
Persepolis early in order to avoid the midday sun. I had been
riding for several hours, and was growing hot and stiff when I
turned a corner in an avenue of trees to see an edifice like the
Wailing Wall. This was Persepolis. Huge blocks of stone five
feet square formed the base of a platform and above rose stark
columns like factory chimneys. A pair of staircases indented one
wall in the shape of a hexagon, and leaving Mephistopheles, I
climbed one side. Four winged bulls, carved onto massive door-
posts, guarded the top, their biceps swelling to a thick-set body.
Their heads were human, surmounted by crowns, and each wore
a beard like a nose-bag. I walked on through rectangular halls, past
corinthian-type capitals and deeply fluted columns. Crenellated
stairways led to different-levelled platforms—the King's apart-
ments, the palace of audience, the Hall of a Hundred Columns.
And blocks of hewn stone formed doorways whose lintels were
carved in lines of stripes.

For this was pre-Islam, pre-Illahs and Allahs, a palace which
was built in the early fifth century, B.C. It was classicism, not
mysticism, and I found it impressive and straightforward, yet

somehow more stolid. Perhaps it was the lack of colour, for with so much stone, it presented a monotone of dull sandy brown.

Throughout, the activities of the court were depicted on the doorways and walls: the king swept by beneath an umbrella; the courtiers chatted, holding hands and lotus flowers; the Immortals lined up, an army whose number was always kept at 10,000, regardless of losses. On the staircases, representatives of the subject nations queued to pay obeisance at the New Year festival; they led rams, bullocks, dromedaries, and bore cloth, precious metals, tanned skins and vessels. There were Egyptians, Assyrians, Babylonians, Abyssinians, plus Indians, Armenians, Phoenicians. Some had cloaks which hung to their calves and some short rustic tunics; many wore hats, including the Sogdians who were redolent of Tolkien's hobbits in pointed funnel caps.

I trudged up and down the steps; but the overhead sun deadened the friezes by flattening their shadows, and by the end of the day I had only two queries. Why were no women shown, and what happened about sewage and water?

Of the harem only the foundations remain, but it surprised me that the queen was not depicted in the activities of the court. Sir Percy Sykes in his *History of Persia* comments with assurance on the position of Achaemenian women:

> Neither in the inscriptions nor in the sculptures does a woman appear . . . jealously guarded, [they] were not even allowed to receive their fathers or brothers. As this has apparently been the general rule in the East, the Persians were no worse off than their neighbours; but their decay as a great empire can be traced in no small degree to the intrigues of eunuchs and women in the *anderun,* as the harem is termed in Persia, where to do any work was degrading.

As for the water, I could trace no baths or pools on the site. But in the base of the platform a complex network of tunnels corresponds exactly with the walls of the palace above. They were used to protect the site during heavy winter rains, for the water was channelled through to them. On the platform itself, unmortared brick drains carried the rainwater off the roofs and along the floors before emptying into the underground network.

It is possible that the tunnels were also used for water supplies, for stone stairways lead down to them, serving both cleaners and carriers. And a cistern, about a hundred yards from the walls, and filled by the winter rains, probably contributed to the court's supply. In the south-east corner of the palace, a small water tank was used for immediate needs. In any case, the Achaemenian kings always took water with them from the river at Susa, when they moved from palace to palace. It was boiled and stored in silver flasks which were carried in wagons drawn by oxen.

The removal of sewage was less hygienic, for the drains of the garrison at Persepolis emptied into the street, and this was probably the case for most other buildings. It seems the Achaemenians paid little attention to their knowledge that flies carried disease from dirt.

Nowadays Persepolis is used for the Shiraz Festival, and the night I was there, a concert was attended by the Empress and élite. Dressed in jewels, bri-nylon, fur wraps, and cotton, the audience of several hundred streamed up the steps and along a tarpaulin carpet to the tiered benches, their way reddened by flames which surged from two cauldrons. The riff-raff, including myself, stood on the roadside, cheering and waving flags.

For the following year's festival, the British Council in Shiraz was organising an exhibition of Henry Moore sculpture. One of the teachers later told me of his visit to the cultural officer:

'I'm most grateful to you for giving me your time,' said the teacher.

'It is an honour,' replied the cultural officer.

'Well, to get to the point, I gather the Ministry in Tehran has agreed to help sponsor the Henry Moore exhibition for the festival.'

'Henry who?'

'Henry Moore, an English sculptor. I've brought some pictures of his work in this book by Thames & Hudson.'

'Aaah . . . Thames, yes, that great English river. But not as big as our Zayendeh Rud?'

'I don't know about that. Yes, I'm sure you're right. But about this Henry Moore exhibition.'

'More? More exhibitions? But we have no exhibitions.'

'But that's why I'm here. The Ministry in Tehran did say it was writing to you to say it was willing to help.'

'I have heard nothing.'

'Oh dear. But I assure you they're agreeable. You see, they have the exhibition in Tehran at the moment.'

'What exhibition? Who wants to show?'

'We do, I mean the British Council together with the Iranian Government . . . an exhibition by Henry Moore.'

'Henry who?' asked the cultural officer, and fingered the pages of the book with a beautifully manicured index finger.

The administrative success of the Achaemenians owed much to communications: roadways and staging posts filled the empire, including a 1500-mile highway from Susa to Sardis. It was covered in two weeks by mounted messenger, but when I returned to Shiraz, I could not match such speed, even with tarmac roads. And I was nearly defeated by the steepest hill, when I had to push Mephistopheles up. He was heavy and I kept stopping for breath and to wash out my mouth with water from my warm plastic bottle. The road was under construction and heavy machinery disturbed the earth into clouds of dust. I longed for a lorry to give me a lift, but the traffic was merciless in edging me into the bank and coating me with dirt. Finally I reached the top and free-wheeled down, gulping the fresh air. But I was disheartened, for if Mephistopheles could not manage this hill, he would certainly not take me into the mountains of the Qashqai tribe.

A few miles on, I saw a hut surrounded by pine trees, where some men were sitting languorously at a table scattered with empty glasses. I manœuvred the bike between the trees, jumped over a channel of water and walked into the hut to see a man heaving lumps of meat out of a tall refrigerator. He turned, and his face dimpled with a smile.

'You want kebab?'

'Thank you, no, just tea.'

'You want yoghourt, or fruit?' He pointed to some grapes which were khaki in colour.

'Just tea, thank you.'

He put down the meat on the table and sighed.

'Always everyone asks just for tea. And what about this meat of mine, a prize sheep I killed especially for visitors like you?'

At that moment a child ran in, her face streaked with dirt and

remnants of food. Reaching the table, she saw the meat and poked
it with her fingers.

'Baba, is this the meat that man gave you for the paraffin?'
The man frowned at her.

'Well Mama says she knows the man had two sick sheep. Do
you think this meat is sick too?'

The man ushered me out and told me to sit with the men. One
of them pulled up a chair and with an oily rag wiped the crumb-
scattered seat. Another offered me a cigarette, and asked:

'Have you come far on that?' And he jerked his thumb at
Mephistopheles.

'Only from Persepolis.'

'Eeeh, you mean Takht-e-Jamshid?'

The palace is known as the throne of Jamshid, the legendary
king whose spies, tradition says, used the sub-terranean tunnels.
One of the tunnels led to a well so deep that an object thrown in
would emerge in the sea three days later.

The man picked his wide nostrils with thumb and forefinger,
then scratched the back of his neck. He was thick-set, with short
legs and heavy boots.

'I'm Mohammad,' he said and cracked each finger. 'This here
is my friend, Hasan.'

Hasan's boniness showed through his clothes, and his cheekbones stuck out like knobs. Round his head was a strip of brown
cloth, tied above his left ear. He saw me looking at it, so lifted the
bandage. A three-inch gash ran across his forehead, its edges
blackened with blood. I grimaced, shutting my eyes, and he burst
into laughter.

'Holy prophets, this young man hates the sight of a wound.' And
running his finger over the scab, he replaced the bandage.

'How on earth did you get it?' I asked.

'This Mohammad here. He was taking a corner and . . . yaaaah
. . . he tried to send us to heaven.'

All the men laughed noisily, slapping their thighs, but Mohammad said indignantly:

'Curses on the devil, *you* can't get to Mecca. Why God made
you a driver—He gave you no skill.'

'To Mecca indeed? I'd beat you any day. And I'd run this boy
off his feet.' He looked at me mockingly.

'I'm afraid I don't know the way,' I said meekly.

'Oh I'll help you with that,' said Hasan, and looking at the sun, he pointed south-west. 'It's over there. Just keep going, and you'll soon arrive—maybe in six months on that bike?'

'And will you take me as a passenger?' scoffed Mohammad.

'No, I'm afraid you're too heavy.' And I added, casually, 'It only takes my wife.'

'Your wife?'

'Yes. And our child.'

Everyone looked at me with astonishment.

'But where are they?' asked Mohammad.

'I left them at home. I mean with this heat, what could I do with them?'

He nodded glumly. 'True, they'd only annoy you. But is she beautiful?'

'Like the moon. And she cooks like . . .' I closed my eyes and threw a kiss to the air.

'You have luck, my friend,' said Mohammad. 'But soon, at the rate I drive, *I'll* have enough money for the ripest fruit in Iran. Then I'll have fifteen children.'

An hour later, I emerged from the bare rust hills to see Shiraz laid out below me. A triumphal arch straddled the road in a complex of latticework and niches, and when I drove down, the town seemed spacious, light-hearted. The backdrop of mountains gave dimension, and destroyed the feeling of oppression, so frequent in desert towns where the sky is cut to a strip by high mud walls. Here, the houses were surrounded by cypress trees and large gardens; through open gateways I glimpsed balconies and flowers —not heavy, fleshy ones, but feathery, long-stemmed and many headed.

But as I explored the town, I felt, as I had done with Isfahan, that the reputation and image far exceeded the reality. Where were the roses and nightingales? True, there were cypress trees, but where was the wine, and the poetry of the place? Perhaps the wide tarmac roads, the hotel blocks, the huge new hospital, were now poetry to the Shirazis, but it was not my idea of Persian poetry.

So I paid my respects to the tombs of Hafiz and Sa'di,* two of Iran's most famous poets, both of whom came from Shiraz. The

* Sa'di died in 1292, Hafiz in 1390.

mausoleums sat in neat gardens, the buildings recently renovated for tourists and pilgrims. Kufic script screamed from coloured walls to convince those who could not read that the poet was illustrious. Men stood intoning the words from the walls, or reciting a passage by heart; women and children kissed the tomb, and ran their hands over the writing.

I sat on some steps in the garden of Hafiz' tomb and pulled out a book which contained some of his work.

> When the wine sun fills the bowl of the East,
> It brings to her cheeks a thousand anemones.
> The wind breaks ringlets of hyacinth
> Over the heads of the roses,
> As among the meadows I inhale
> The fragrance of her rich hair.
> This does not express the night of separation,
> For the fragments of her explanation
> Would fill a hundred books.*

Now I was in Iran, I could understand this poetry more, the flamboyant addresses, the mystical undertones. For such imagery has been defended by a Persian Sufi author, so that wine may mean ecstatic experience with God; kisses, Godly rapture; beauty, the perfection of God. If this is so, then how magnificently Hafiz unites the sublime with the erotic without debasing either:

> Her hair in disarray, lips laughing;
> Drunk in the sweat of revelry
> Singing of love, she came, flask in hand.
>
> Dishevelled and her clothes rent
> Last midnight by my bed she bent;
> Her lips curved in regret.
>
> I saw sorrow quarrel in her eyes
> As her whispers spoke softly,
> 'Is our old love asleep?'

* Trs. R. M. Rehder. *Anthology of Islamic Literature* (ed. Kritzech), London 1967. First pub. Holt, Rinehart & Winston Inc, New York 1964

Given such a wine before dawn,
A lover is an infidel to love
If he does not drink.

Wine, the famous wine of Shiraz—I could not find it anywhere,
and I thought how Jesus Christ would have laughed in Qum if he
knew how the laws of Mohammad had thwarted me. Only before
the invasion of Islam did a Chinese general remark on the Persians'
love for wine, and their horses' love for lucerne. And so delighted
was he that he took cuttings back to China.

Instead of wine I found lemon juice and syrup, in shops that
replaced the normal *chai khane*. Each place I visited had a row of
metal chairs, and every wall was lined with litre bottles of lemon
juice. In one corner were crates of more bottles, where the proprietor, or his son, or his grandson, were sticking on the shop's
label. Behind a partition were tumblers and syrups, murky yellow,
vermilion, lime green.

Much of the lemon juice is produced in factories, but once I saw
it made by hand. A brawny man, his legs wide apart clutching a
small mesh-topped table, thundered down with a rolling pin on
one small lemon to crush out its stomach; and as the juice dripped
through the table, the deft hand of a boy snatched away the
crumpled body and replaced it with a pregnant one.

There was a glut of fruit in Shiraz, and barrowfuls of melons
lined the roads. The first pomegranates lay in piles beside seedless
grapes; pears, apples, peaches and apricots grew mushy in the heat,
to be picked over by stooping women. There was dried fruit, too—
full-blown dates like horse-chestnut buds; figs, their shrivelled
bodies threaded on string like a carved bead necklace; and other
fruits, unidentifiable in their leathery non-shapes which were piled
into sacks.

Fruit, white salted cheese, half a slab of unleavened bread, an
oil rag, some cheap cigarettes, and my water-bottle, filled one side
of my saddle-bag as I bumped south-east out of Shiraz one
morning, heading for Firuzabad, the winter headquarters of the
Qashqai tribe. It was cool at that hour, six o'clock, and the jaded
light of the street lamps was competing with the freshening sky.
I had left my jersey in Tehran, forgetting that summer was turning
to autumn, and I kept my arms together to ward off the wind.

Small trucks and bicycles were already on the road, making their way to the orchards and outlying fields; and men were cutting corn, scything their way in rows down the yellow expanse. Much of the land was cultivated, but as I went further, the soil deteriorated and was strewn with rocks; the houses were fewer, the villages were scattered. It was the beginning of tribal country.

I came to a police road check, and they suggested I turn back. I continued, but the gradients grew until I was stopping frequently for rest. Then the road shrank to a dusty track and disappeared in contortions up the side of a mountain. I raced up the approach, kept the accelerator open, pedalled standing up, cursed my aching thighs, got off, pushed the bike, and finally sat down. I continued for an hour, with minimal progress, as the hill grew more aggressive, and the bike heavier. My body protested with cupfuls of sweat; my mouth worked the air like sandpaper. Red in the face from exertion, I dropped Mephistopheles on his side and slumped against a rock. With mortification I realised I would have to return to Shiraz. I sat for a few minutes and then, remounting the bike, I rattled back down the hill. I hardly noticed the oncoming lorry, which braked, spewed out its yelling occupants, ingurgitated five grinning men, one person sex unknown, one moped, and continued snorting on its way.

We jolted up, up through the mountains in a posse of dust and heat. Scrub bushes swam dizzily across the hillside, and an eagle circled against the ceiling of sky—only some tribesmen were needed to tomahawk their way through us. Or would this hurtling band of brigands take the opportunity first and remove my teeth for gold stoppings, gouge out my eyes to sell at market, strip me of my clothes and so find something else to use? I laughed manfully, slapped them on the back and breathed more freely as we tipped down towards the bottom of a shallow bowl where I hoped for the security of habitation. I was disappointed. There was no house nor human anywhere, only signs of the living in the cream area of stubble, crossed and recrossed by red dust tracks, where unaccompanied sheep made paths to nowhere. The unreality of the scene, focused by the encirclement of hills, was intense as the engine suddenly stopped. The men got out and beckoned me to follow.

'Oh Lord,' I thought, though with so many Muslims near me,

He was unlikely to hear my prayer. 'Why should I get out?' I asked.

'Why, because we . . .' The explanation was lost in their gabble.

'No, thank you. I'm in a hurry to reach Firuzabad.' I tapped my watch.

They eyed it. 'How much is it?'

'It's very bad. Broken. I have very little.' I indicated my saddle-bag. They saw my camera, a fat Nikkormat, bulging out of the top, and told me to come down.

'But I must reach Firuzabad this afternoon, soon, because . . .' My words were incoherent, for what reason does one have for arriving on time in a remote place where the hour is calculated by the sun and the stomach?

They told me again to get down, so I did. We stepped off the road and disappeared behind a large rock. Fear was hammering at my throat, and I felt like being sick. Then I noticed the men, rather than pulling out knives, were pulling down their trousers. They were going to urinate. But still I was in difficulty for I could not participate without revealing my sex. So, with a cry, I bent to the ground, picked up some pebbles and ran to the lorry, where I pretended to study them intently. The men's gaze followed my movements and then, shaking their heads, they turned idly back and completed their work.

My identity did not remain concealed once I reached Firuzabad, for the village supported a cumulation of gendarmes who made every unco-ordinated effort to check my passport, each time I left and returned to the village. Word soon spread that I was a girl and when I was in the streets, men cupped imaginary breasts and swayed their hips provocatively at me.

I reported at the gendarmerie for my documents to be examined. Within minutes, the place was crowded with officers comparing my physique with my passport photograph. A doctor was called, not as I expected to verify my sex but because he spoke English. He took me to his home, introducing me as a boy to his wife, and after lunch, he said:

'Sweet girl, shall we take our siesta in the next room? Don't be embarrassed, my wife suspects nothing. We can have beautiful hours together.'

I refused, and with a belch, he left the room to sleep by himself.

His wife, Malake, brought tea, bowing as she gave it to me, and when I asked her to have some too, she sat on the carpet, tucking her feet under her short black shirt. She was plump, with full breasts and a protruding stomach which made her skirt wrinkle at her thighs; her black nylon shirt was unbuttoned at the neck. The room was hot so that her face glistened with perspiration and her oily skin looked sallow from lack of contact with fresh air; her eyes were small, the eyelashes coated with mascara; and the nose was flat, accentuating the darkness of her upper lip.

It was the first time I had been alone with a woman, indeed the first time I had dared to look in detail at one under fifty. But whether I was studying her as a boy or a girl I did not know, though I wondered if she made love well.

Malake picked up a box, opened it and handed it to me.

'Please, would you like a cigarette?'

'Thank you.' I took one and lit it. 'That was an excellent lunch you gave us. You cook very well.' I accepted quite easily her role as preparer of food.

She smiled. 'I'm glad. It's difficult to buy good food here, but we manage.'

'Do you like it here?'

She shrugged. 'It's remote. It's also difficult. Many of the women don't approve of me. They think I'm too free without the veil. And my husband doesn't let me mix with his friends, so really I see few people.'

She fetched a plate of sweets, placing them by me.

'Please, take some,' she said, and watched as I ate. 'You must eat more. You're thin. Don't you have a wife to cook for you?'

'Not yet,' I said. 'I like the freedom.'

'But my husband is free, even though he's got me. He's very clever, you know. He reads lots of books—he's making me learn English.'

She pulled from a shelf an illustrated textbook and read out slowly: ' "Today it is raining, and I put on my mackintosh." ' Then she gave me the book: 'My husband reads the hardest passages.'

I flicked through to see exercises on electricity and fox-hunting.

'Do you read?' she asked.

'Yes, a bit.'

'Philosophy? Medicine? You must be very clever. My husband says I'm very stupid. I know so little.'

She sat in silence, looking down at the carpet. Then I heard outside the beat of a drum and the noise of a crowd.

'What's happening?'

'I don't know.'

'Then let's go and see.'

We walked out of the house and crossed the street. A number of men had gathered in the dusty grounds of a school, to watch two men fighting and dancing in ritual. Armed with sticks, they tried to hit each other below the knee, making vibrant gestures to the noise of a drum and tin trumpet. Each time a hit was made, the vanquished left the field and another contestant took his place. After a few bouts, I was pushed into the circle of men and given a stick. My opponent was frightening, a tall, wiry man with muscular limbs and a supple body. But spurred on by the hand-clapping, and disregarding unsportingly the few rules I had noted, I managed to hit his thighs with a thwack. It was obvious he had let me do it, but the onlookers cheered enthusiastically, and making a deep bow, I walked off in glory with the doctor's wife on my arm. How easy, I thought, to have been a knight.

When we returned, the doctor was awake and Malake recounted my exploits. He laughed so uncontrollably that she questioned him.

'Why, you simpleton, this boy's a girl, and she's won in a game that only men play.'

Malake swung round to study me. 'Of course, that explains it.'

'Explains what?' I asked.

'Why you didn't move much during the fight. You were frightened of even lifting your arms. But come, sit down, and I'll make some tea.'

Later the doctor went to visit some patients. Malake moved herself closer to me and whispered confidentially, now that she knew I was a woman:

'You know, I've just had a miscarriage.'

'Oh, I'm sorry, it must have been terrible for you.'

'Yes, I was sad. I'm longing for children. It might bring my husband closer.' She brushed an invisible speck from her skirt. 'He's often away.'

'Can't you go with him?'

'Oh no, that's impossible, I must look after the house. Besides I don't know how much he wants me. Not even for children.'

'Don't worry, Malake,' I said, not knowing either. 'He probably just can't think of children yet. His work's preoccupying him, that's all.'

She smiled wryly. 'Well, I suppose you should know, Miss John.'

I used Firuzabad as a base to explore the surrounding districts where many Qashqai had pitched their tents on return from their summer pastures. For each spring they migrate some three hundred miles to the mountains to find grazing for their flocks. There they remain through the summer, high up, tending their sheep, planting crops, weaving, hunting, making butter and cheese. And in the autumn, they plant wheat for the following year, then return to the plains for winter.

The migration is complex and highly organised, with an intricate schedule of movement. Each group sets off with orders to follow a definite route. If the grazing is good, they take six weeks; if sparse, they hurry for home. And as there are thousands of Qashqai, the hillsides and plains swarm with people. The tribe itself is divided into sub-tribes, each with its leader, and those sub-tribes are further divided into groups of tents.

Many tents were scattered round Firuzabad, their shapes black against the white earth, with the loose weave pitched on knock-kneed poles for ceiling and wall. One encampment was near the ruins of a Sassanian castle, silent in the shimmering heat where sheep nibbled wearily. Only women were there, wearing their long petticoats of vivid gauze beneath heavy tabards. On their heads, a long silk scarf bound a filmy white square.

Two of them, their skirts hooped round them, were squatting on the earth, weaving a strip of brown tent material. A young girl was suckling a child from wrinkled and sagging breasts; others were stoking a fire and cooking, while an old lady, rocking on her heels, chanted some tale or love-story, or perhaps a vilification against the neighbouring tent.

I approached the group warily, not wishing to intrude. They nodded curtly, not speaking, but one of the younger girls pulled a rug off a pile at the back of the tent, unrolled it and told me to sit down. She gave me some tea, and then continued weaving. Their curiosity was refreshingly negative, their coyness non-existent, and when I asked questions, their answers were short. I could understand nothing of their chatter, for the Qashqai use a Turkish dialect though they can speak Persian: it is claimed they came with the Mongols under Hulagu Khan, and moved from the Caucasus some three hundred years ago to Fars.

While I was sitting watching the women, one of the men came into the camp with two dogs at his heels. The moment he saw me, he strode to our tent. The dogs growled, sniffing the ground where I had walked, but withdrew when a child threw stones at them.

'Where are you from?' asked the man in Persian.

'From Firuzabad,' I answered.

'Have you seen all you want?' He frowned and his scalp moved forward. He was wearing a tribal felt hat, moulded into a dome and guarded at the sides by wide upright flaps. Once flesh pink, it was now brown from dirt and sweat, and, shrunk by the rain, it squeezed his forehead.

I got up to leave and he followed me to Mephistopheles.

'How were the mountains?' I asked.

'Dry,' he grunted. 'No grazing. Driest we've had for years.'

'So you came back early?'

'Had to. They gave us permission for once.'

'They' are the Tribal Office, who have increasing control. Once the tribes were politically active—they deposed the Shah in 1909 through rebellion, and in 1946 defeated the Iranian Communist party. But now they are disarmed, induced to settle, and their movements are firmly restricted.

I got on Mephistopheles and started the engine. The man studied him.

'Not much good,' I said. 'It won't get me up the mountains.'

'You'd do better with one of our camels,' he answered. 'They cross anything and need no petrol.'

South of Firuzabad lies a narrow but deep valley, hemmed in on three sides and leading to a gorge which gives protected access to the residence of one of the Qashqai leaders. Within the valley are small hamlets, walled in and filled with flat-topped mud houses, and from one to the other runs a maze of paths. I came to the first village to find a group of tribesmen clustered outside the walls.

They watched without expression as I passed, and one called to ask if I knew where I was going.

It was early morning. Down on the right, either side of a much reduced stream, a narrow strip of bean fields lay waiting to be worked. Above, the hills were gathering colour as the rays of the sun pierced the valley. Grey boulders and knobs of land diminished into far-off lumps and paths wound into the distance like the tracing of a pencil. Figures on donkeys moved out from the buildings, escorting their cattle or sheep to the stream.

I progressed down the valley and when the sun slid into the open, I sat on a rock to warm myself. I could hear the clink of a sheep-bell quite near and soon a flock came into view. It was followed by a man astride a donkey, his legs hanging directly down from his body and joggling with the movements of the animal. His bare feet nearly touched the ground, though occasionally one was lifted to prompt the donkey's belly. He passed in front of my rock, and nodded.

'Peace be upon you,' I offered.

'And peace upon you, too,' he returned.

'May the morning of your noble person be good.'

'To your kindness.'

I was smoking a cigarette, so drew out my packet and offered him one. He dismounted, and taking it, sucked at the end and then sat down beside me, leaving his sheep to wander. I lit a match and his hands moved to protect the flame. They were bony hands, with heavily lined skin and cracked nails; grey hairs curled over the wrists. His back was straight, his shoulder-blades defined clearly through his shirt.

'The day is beautiful,' I said.

'Allah is good,' came the response. Allah is always good, it seems, even when your prize cow dies.

'Are these your sheep?' I asked.

'They are my wife's sister's husband's. All these.' His arm encompassed the fifteen sheep.

'The grazing is sufficient?'

'God willing, there is enough.'

We sat in silence, each puffing out smoke and considering the day. For him, it was probably God's day, the same as any other day, ruled by the sun and the need to find fresh pasture, but filled with worry of how to feed his family and how to find money for a new felt hat. For my part, I took in the stillness and wondered how I should survive such a life.

'Have you always lived here?' I asked.

'No, I used to go to the mountains each summer. But now I stay in the village over there.' He pointed to a cluster of mud dwellings.

The settled and nomadic Qashqai are not mutually exclusive, and if conditions or the urge demand, those who have settled may join the trek. And through loss of flocks, or accumulated wealth, some of the nomads choose to settle; others are forced by government pressures.

The old man stood up. 'Please, go to my village. Bread has just been baked.'

'I shall be glad.' I also stood up and we shook hands.

'May God be your protector.'

'In the protection of God, farewell.'

I took the old man's advice and came to a miniature plateau which supported the village and cattle compound. Men and women were sorting and taking away their cattle to the whine of a machine, a Heath Robinson affair which was worked by three men. They were grinding corn and most of the flour spun onto them and the ground.

I left Mephistopheles against the village wall, and walked down a narrow alley. Some children rushed up, to cling to my arms and to pat my stomach-pouch. They were barefoot, with threadbare clothes, but they looked healthy and their eyes gleamed. They took me into a dark room whose dry mud walls were decorated with crumpled newspaper pictures. A tribal rug covered the floor. I was surprised for the village was poor: carpets indicate a man's wealth, just as the size of the Shah's statue in the reception roundabout indicate a town's wealth. Perhaps it was the house of the village weaver; or perhaps it belonged to the local prostitute.

It was a loosely-knotted rug that gave the feeling of lightness, with a burnt orange background offsetting chocolate, claret and white. Angular scrollwork severed the border, while a mixture of flowers, and patterns like haircombs, swept in to a central medallion. I found it beautiful, with its juxtaposition of straight line and curvature: it was Persia and the Caucasus combined.

One of the older children brought in some cheese, tea and hot bread, and when I offered them some, they turned their backs in refusal. I saw a woman peering through the doorway. Her skin was rough like hessian, and her slender figure meant a shortage of skirts, thus money.

'Did you provide the meal?' I asked.

She nodded.

'But I must pay for it. How much do I owe you?'

'You owe me nothing.'

'Of course I do. Let me give you something.'

Her head went back, her tongue clicked in refusal. 'We need nothing.' And she moved away.

That day, the division of time into minutes and hours seemed meaningless as I enquired into one molecule of the earth's composition. There was nothing to distract me or press me as I stopped to take in the slenderness of one grass stem, or to study the shape of an insect's mouth. The valley turned from the greenish yellow of early morning to the monochrome beige of midday. The villages, more scattered now, became silent. The sky was static, then gradually through the afternoon faded to a gentle blue. I turned back, and passing the same villages, saw the cattle brought in for the night. I thought I had gone many miles, but moving continuously, I reached Firuzabad within two hours.

The following morning I moved eastwards and came to a walled garden filled with orange trees and cypresses. I sat in the dust beside a muddy stream to peel one of the oranges: it was unripe and bitter so I took a pomegranate from my saddle-bag and munched the flesh-covered pips. Next to the garden was a school, a corrugated hut of two rooms with broken windows. There was no-one about for it was holiday time, so I peered in. I could imagine unkindly the term-time scene: both rooms crowded with children of varying ages, several chanting arithmetic tables, others reading aloud from one textbook, a few painfully copying letters from the blackboard.

The nomads themselves have tent schools which move with the migrations; they are visible for miles, white specks in the group of black tents. And in order to lessen resentment of official intrusion in education the teachers are Qashqai: they train probably in Shiraz, and then join their own tribal group.

Tribal Interlude

I moved on into the hills, and found a narrow track which led through a ravine: some camels were grazing nearby and a solitary black tent guarded the entrance. Within a few minutes, walls of rock rose either side of me to shut out most of the sky and to throw back the noise of the motorbike. Three spiky trees sentinelled the route and a bird high above cawed eerily. Then the ravine widened slightly, narrowed again between a promontory of rock and relaxed into a valley. Scrub bushes undulated with the ground to stop suddenly at a cliff edge. Below ran miles of plateau, incised with rifts and half-submerged hills. The track dropped down, clinging to the cliff face, and fearing Mephistopheles would not re-ascend, I descended on foot. It was strange country, almost surreal, with twisted contours and Daliesque vegetation, where angular bushes contorted dimensions and flimsy shadows seemed uncertain where to lie.

I clapped my hands. The noise bounced back, bounced back, off the cliff face, to be followed by cries of 'Good, good, good'. I sat down. There was silence. Nothing moved; there was not a dwelling or animal in sight. Perhaps this was tribal hunting country, not fit for habitation. Perhaps it was just waste-land, ruled by snakes and scorpions, where even antelope feared to come. How long, I wondered, would I survive here alone. Apart from the problems of food and water, would I soon need the company of people? The support, say, of a tribal community, whose members, though fiercely independent, seldom went anywhere by themselves. And might this land, which now I found so impressive, finally become oppressive?

Though I was happy to follow peacefully wherever the tracks led, I felt I must make an effort to study more the designs of the Qashqai; and after some enquiry, I was told of a woman who made carpets in a nearby village. It was a small village, and I had no difficulty in finding her house, for it was the only one with a corrugated roof. I knocked on the gate, and when a voice called 'Welcome', I walked in. A young woman was sitting on the pebbled floor of a small yard, a narrow loom stretched out in front of her. Above, a canopy of branches and dried leaves protected her from the sun. She was wearing a skirt patterned in pinks and reds, and her loose blouse glistened with gold thread. A long scarlet scarf was tied at the back of her dark hair, and round her neck were strings of gold coins.

She looked up and smiled.

'The peace of God be with you,' I said.

'His mercies always rest with you,' she replied. Her face was oval, with a long straight nose, the skin was smooth, and the lids of her eyes were darkened.

'May I watch you work?' I asked, squatting on the pebbles.

She nodded, and pulled at the warps as though playing a harp. Then she began to knot, her fingers working the wool deftly. They were supple hands, with the ends of the fingers and thumbs curving backwards.

After a few minutes she leant back so that I could see the design. Large rhomboids inset with diamonds were fringed with 'L' shaped lines. Angular flowers linked themselves through the background, and a double border was interlaced with straight-sided scrollwork. But the colours were harsh—bright red, clear navy, white. There was no russet or burnt orange for which the Qashqai were once known.

'Don't you dye your own wools?' I asked.

'I like to get them from Shiraz. They have bright colours there.'

She got up to make some tea, and came back with a trayful of dry biscuits, bread, scarlet jam, and glasses of tea.

'Have you been making carpets long?' I asked.

'All my life. My mother taught me.'

'And what do you use for patterns?'

'She taught me them too. And I copy some of the ones in Shiraz.'

'You like Shiraz?'

She shrugged. 'I can sell my carpets there. For a good price. But it's too busy for me. I usually get my brother to sell them for me—he loves it. Though he goes there little enough. Only on his way to the mountains.'

She began to knot again, and I sat in silence. She seemed unperturbed that a man should be sitting alone with her, but perhaps I looked too young to present a threat. I felt comfortable in her presence, for there seemed to be no male-female issue. We were both human beings with work to do.

She poured out some more tea for me.

'What about your family? You have a family, don't you?' she asked, looking at my filthy shirt.

'Oh yes, but they're in England. What about yours?'

'My husband and sons are away. They're helping my brother bring the sheep home.'

I was surprised that he was with her family, for normally the woman is integrated into the husband's family. But perhaps because of her wealth from carpet-making, he chose to stay with her kindred.

'Come,' she said, standing up. 'I have other carpets to look at.' She led me into the house, stooping as she entered the low doorway. The room was white-washed, and in one corner, hanging over a wooden rod, were petticoats—pastel blue flecked with gold, mauve nylon patterned with fuchsia pink, limes, turquoise, scarlets, yellow. Gaudy colours, maybe, but I found them an exciting relief from the interminable ochre of the landscape.

Some carpets were rolled against one wall, and the woman pulled them out one by one. The patterns were fairly consistent, with the softness of flowers and circular shapes contrasted with angular motifs. But within each one, there was a variation of detail and linking patterns which made it seem individual, almost unrelated to the rest.

'This one's very cheap,' said the woman. 'Or there's this one, which is twice the price. But twice the size.'

I was embarrassed. 'I'm afraid I don't want to buy.'

She looked puzzled. 'Don't you like them?'

'Oh yes, they're beautiful. I just wanted to see them.'

She smiled. 'I'm glad. Perhaps one day you will buy one. I can make one specially for you.'

'Thank you.' I held out my hand. 'May your shadow never grow less.'

'May all the bounties be with you.'

I started Mephistopheles and set off back to Firuzabad. The sun was dropping steadily in front of me, its brightness dazzling my eyes so that I could hardly see. On the right, the edge of the plain soared into a cliff whose face was gouged with crevices, and on the left, a few fires were flickering in front of black tents as preparations began for the evening meal.

Ahead of me was a cloud of dust and the noise of sheep-bells. A large flock was coming towards me, taking up the whole road, so I stopped the bike and waited. Small boys drove the sheep on with sticks, yelling and whistling, and when they saw me coated with dust, they called:

'Are you all right?'

'Fine,' I called back.

'What are you doing here anyway?'

'Just looking. It's good country.'

They clustered round me. 'Do you think so? It's dry though. Where do you come from? Have you got any sheep?'

I laughed. 'I'm from England. It's all green there.'

'Green? All the year? Oh please, come with us. You must tell us about it.'

One boy turned my bike and started pushing it, so I walked along behind. Following the sheep, we turned off the road towards some tents; but Mephistopheles refused to go because of the numbers of rocks which covered the ground.

'We'll leave it,' said the boy, dropping him against a boulder.

'No, please not,' I pleaded, frightened it would be stolen.

'Don't worry, it'll be quite safe. We'll tell everyone it's there. Then no-one will dare take it.'

We walked on towards the tents, the boys arguing loudly:

'He's coming to my home.'

'No, he's coming to *mine*.'

'I'm the eldest,' said one with finality.

So we went to his family's tent. His mother and sister were cooking over the fire and when I arrived they immediately began preparing more dishes, calling out in shrill voices for ingredients. The father was sitting at the back of the tent, still in his felt hat, and gazing blankly out towards the plain as he smoked. His face was weather-beaten, and the skin beneath his eyes was crinkled as though he constantly screwed up his eyes against the sun. His fingers were at right-angles to his swollen knuckles, for his tendons had contracted.

We sat down near him and the boys cross-examined me about England, my school, my work. They were sharp-witted and laughed frequently. And when it grew dark one of them lit a hurricane lamp.

Supper came and we sat in a large circle eating from a central dish with our fingers. There was rice and hunks of greasy mutton, hot bread and fresh yoghourt. As each one finished, he belched and moved back against some cushions. We sat in silence, a silence interrupted occasionally by comments which needed no response.

'We must find fresh grazing tomorrow. The split bowl is all used up,' said the old man, drawing on his pipe.

'The black ewe went lame today.'

'Rice costs three *toman* in the bazaar.'

And everyone grunted in agreement. Finally one of the boys got up.

'We must go and look at the sheep.'

Several of us followed him outside, and I took a few minutes to adjust to the darkness. The sky was clear, an indigo lightened by the half moon and swarm of stars. Embers of fires glowed red, and a dog barked as we moved from the tents.

The flock was about two hundred yards away; some of the sheep were coughing, others were grazing still, their bells clinking. As we approached, one boy let out a long whistle. A whistled tune came back in reply, and we soon met up with the shepherd.

'Any troubles?'

'No troubles. The black ewe's leg seems better.'

'Till tomorrow then.' And we returned to the tent.

The women had hung a curtain across one end to form a small compartment, and they were unrolling some bedding on the floor.

'Please, for you,' they said, and pushing me in, they secured the bottom of the curtain with some stones. I wrapped the blankets tightly round me, for it was cold and my breath showed white against the air. The next morning, I woke early to the sound of shouts as the shepherds started the flock moving. I scrambled out of bed, gulped down some tea, said goodbye to the women, and ran after the flock. It was cool still, and the sky was only just beginning to lighten with dawn.

'What's the hurry?' asked the boy whose tent I had stayed in. I slowed down immediately, and laughed at my haste.

'My bike,' I said, shamefacedly. 'I can't remember where we left it.'

The boy looked at me accusingly, as though I had no right to be in a country where it was elementary to remember the relationship of boulders and gullies.

'We'll come to it,' he said, and when we did, he pushed the sheep past it, and said an abrupt farewell. The other boys passed by, and shouting at the flock, gave me a cursory nod.

I was beginning to grow angry with Mephistopheles, for he refused to go up anything more than a gentle slope; and as my main purpose was to go deep into the mountains, it seemed he had ruined my plans. I therefore determined to go back to Shiraz by bus, and start off again from there.

When we reached the city, many Qashqai were camping on the outskirts, resting and stocking up with food and water before the final stretch home. Sheep strayed onto private property or confused themselves with cars; tents cluttered the view of factories, and children made cars swerve as they chased a donkey across the road. In the bazaar, men haggled over the price of scarlet gauze which they had chosen for their wife's next petticoat, and a few were selling to dealers the work of the summer: carpets and saddlebags, wool and carved sticks.

On the road west, I could sense the antagonism between traffic and tribesmen. For the groups of Qashqai had taken the tarmac road as the quickest and easiest route through the hills, but it meant that nothing else could pass. Streams of sheep filled the road, followed by shepherds, burdened donkeys, camels with tentpoles awry on their backs, and horses caparisoned with petticoated women. Throughout men were guiding the animals, and children ran in and out of the group.

Further up the hill, a bus appeared and sounded its horn to clear the road, but none of the tribesmen moved. At two hundred yards, and gathering speed, the bus blared again. No concession was made. Then there was a squeal of brakes, and the bus jerked to a halt: red faces and fists appeared at the windows and the driver invoked the wrath of God on every living nomad. Giving no acknowledgement, except the space of the bus, the party marched on.

The groups grew more sparse as I continued on Mephistopheles, wheeling through a range of mountains on hot tarmac; and when the road became a dust track, there was not one group to provide relief of colour. It was a grim scene, as though suffering from war rather than road-contractors, a desolate stretch of flat country with burnt-out spikes of vegetation and heavily truncated trees whose foliage was disguised by dust. Heavy machinery was tearing the ground to widen the road from here to the Persian Gulf for better communications, and not until Bishapur did I leave the noise and dirt.

It was here that the Sassanian Shapur I built a palace in the third century, A.D., and carved his triumphs in rock along the valley edge. I wanted to see particularly how these rock carvings illustrated the fabrics of robes; for weaving, especially of silk and brocade, was one of the Sassanians' main industries, and they developed complex and symbolic designs which influenced both early Islamic patterns and Byzantine fabrics.

First I looked at the palace. It was hard to imagine from the ruins of rubble the aura and pomp which surrounded their kings, when anyone approaching had to cover his nose with a handkerchief for fear of contaminating the royal personage. Like the Qajars, the Sassanian kings excelled in their sovereignty. Tradition says that Khusrau II,* apart from his 3000 women, 1000 elephants, and 8500 horses for riding, had a backgammon board made of coral and turquoise, a block of gold so soft he could mould it, and a napkin he threw in the fire to clean—probably made of asbestos.

Near the palace stands part of a fortress on the summit of a hill, its arches and walls searing the sky. At its base were some hovels, made with rough stones or a covering of twigs. And it reminded me that alongside the Sassanian sumptuousness there was abject poverty. Even the personal physician of one of the kings was prompted to comment:

> These times, which have become old and decrepit, seem pure but in reality are turbid. For if God has given joy and success to the King, if the King is at the same time wise, all powerful, magnanimous, profound, humane . . . we see that despite this, our time is in decadence everywhere . . . that what is good withers and what is bad grows green, that wrongs advance laughing, that good conduct draws back crying . . . It is as if the world, drunk with joy, was saying: I have shut away what is good and released to the day what is bad.†

* Reigned A.D. 590–628.
† Translated from A. Christensen, *L'Iran sous les Sassanides*, Copenhagen 1944.

In the valley beyond the fortress, I came to the rock carvings. They were badly damaged, but I could see Shapur I gloating over the Roman Emperor Valerian, after his conquest in A.D. 260. The figures seemed clumsy and lifeless to me, but the folds of their robes swirled about their legs with a grace and movement unexpected in the solid rock. I was surprised that most of the material was undecorated, for it is certain that Sassanian cloth was lavishly patterned with religious animals and plants, and enriched with jewels and gold. Such fabric was used by the nobility for luxurious garments, for wall-hangings, carpets and tents.

And of all garments, the page of Khusrau II said the most useful was one which '. . . for Spring is made of cloth from Merv or Dabiq; for Summer, from material from Tauwaz or Shata; for Autumn, with double weave from Rayy, or a mixed cloth from Merv; for Winter, material woven from wool and silk, or furs made from the skin of cormorant; for the icy days, a garment of silk and wool lined with the same fabric with a heavy silk in between.'*

Through the centre of the valley twisted a river, watering citrus groves and fields. I pushed Mephistopheles over slimy pebbles and followed the track to a village. It seemed Mediterranean in character, with low stone walls and white-washed houses. Through the village ran a wide channel of water, its sides cemented, its base waving with weeds and fish. Some boys were swimming, and diving off a sewage pipe, and when I sat down to eat my lunch, one scrambled out to come and sit beside me.

'Hello, sir, how are you?' he said in English.

'Peaceful, thank you.'

'Please, come and swim.'

'I've nothing to swim in.'

'Don't worry, you can swim without anything.'

'Well, in fact I can't swim.'

'Aaah,' he said, and did two press-ups to show off his strength. He rolled onto his back and picked his teeth.

'You are French, yes?'

'No, I'm English.'

'England is bad, no?'

* Translated from A. Christensen, *L'Iran sous les Sassanides*, Copenhagen 1944.

'No. Why?'

'No God, many divorce, men and women . . . eeeh.' He hooked his forefingers together and screwed up his eyes which were bloodshot from swimming. Then he examined me. 'You are married?'

'No, not yet.'

'But you have women?'

'No.'

The boy looked pleased. 'You have men, then?'

'Not that either.'

He looked puzzled. 'But you must have something if you come from England.'

I leant back against the stones and closed my eyes, hoping he would go away. The boy continued:

'Iran good country. We have many schools, many pupils. We are a great nation. And what will I be? I will be a great electrician, very rich. And I will have two televisions.'

I thought sadly how for this boy the importance of tribal unity had disappeared, to be replaced by a positive, and mercenary nationalism. Soon, no doubt, this would be so with most of the tribesmen, who would lose the protection, the solidity, of a self-contained community.

I continued along the valley on Mephistopheles, for I knew that a large statue of Shapur was in a cave somewhere along the hillside. I passed two men on their donkeys, and because the petrol was low, I stopped further on to refill the tank. I turned to unscrew the cap and thought the back looked different: my saddlebag was missing. I sped back over the track, to find nothing, though I remembered tying it on when I left the river. I came to the two men on their donkeys, and they moved to one side to let me past.

'Have you seen a saddle-bag?' I asked eagerly.

'What saddle-bag?' asked the older man.

'Mine, it's dropped off my bike.'

'We have seen nothing.'

Something made me say: 'I think you have.' But I could not see it on their donkeys.

The man looked surly. 'We've seen nothing. What would we want with a saddle-bag?'

I persisted in my accusations. Finally, he slid off his donkey and went behind a knoll, returning with my bag.

'We were protecting it from thieves for you.'

'Then why didn't you give it me sooner?'

'We had to make sure it was yours.'

I took it and tied it firmly to Mephistopheles. Starting the engine, I moved forward. But the donkeys blocked my way.

'We've done you great service, and saved you much money,' said the man, holding out his hand.

I pulled out five *toman*.

'The two of us have saved your property.'

I pulled out another five *toman*. He took it, and touching his head called out as I passed:

'Your favour is great.'

'May your hands not pain you your effort,' I called back.

Twenty miles from Bishapur lies Kazerun, the 'Northampton of Persia', as one nineteenth-century traveller remarked on purchasing a pair of leather slippers there. It is a neglected place, for the main road now by-passes it, and an air of inertia seeps through. But I found it charming, more like a coastal town, with white sand and palm trees, and the smell of salt pervading; I discovered fish to eat, the only time in Iran, coloured with saffron to hide its decay, and turkish delight stuck with walnuts.

I decided to make the town my base, and my first day's expedition took me into the mountains above Kazerun. There was no habitation, nor sheep, only paths leading into red cliffs and one bent man picking grasses and herbs. I discovered little but learnt, through sweating, how to form marbled patterns on the seat of my trousers. When I dropped down to the town again, it was beginning to rise from its afternoon stupor and several men blinked befuddledly as I entered a dim, smoke-filled *chai khane*. My hair and eyebrows were whitened by dust, my face was flushed from the heat, and my throat rasped. I drank three pints of water, then ordered a large bowl of yoghourt to desalt my mouth.

The following day I drove southwards. Wheat was being tossed by men and women on threshing platforms along the roadside, the chaff misting till dispersed by the breeze. Sheep jingled in the distance accompanied by the whistle of their keeper, and a hawk settled on a telegraph wire. The air was pungent from date-palms and oleander, and filled with the noise of workers who were laughing in an orchard nearby. Further on was a lake, dotted with white birds, possibly flamingoes. But as I approached to see, Mephistopheles stuck in the white salt flats which surrounded the water. I was about to desert him and walk to the lake when I saw a lorry coming towards the flats. Within moments, a dozen men had gathered round me with bandaged heads and tattered clothes.

'Salaam,' they said, though I doubt if the peace of God was in their minds, and they swamped me with the usual questions.

'What is your name? What is your country? Do you have sisters? Do you have brothers? What is your age? Who are your parents? Give me your picture. What are you doing?'

I was suddenly exasperated by their curiosity, perhaps unfairly for it was only a natural inquisitiveness which so many Iranians seem to have. But for once I wanted to be silent, to reach my lake alone, to have some solitude.

'I'm trying to find a place to boil my kettle for tea,' I said facetiously. 'Would you care to join me?'

'Blessings for your kindness. We would like some tea. But where's the kettle?'

'I left it over there to be filled with rain.' I pointed to the barren flats.

'Rain? Is it coming?' And the man looked up to the sky.

'But where are you going?' asked another.

'To America,' I answered relentlessly.

They all nodded at the wisdom of my plan, but the same man was perplexed.

'On that?' he asked, pointing to Mephistopheles.

'It floats,' I explained. 'But unfortunately it doesn't fly. It's stuck at the moment you see.'

One man got on Mephistopheles, and starting him, tried to move him. But he would not budge. Then five others gathered round and picking him up, carried him unceremoniously back to the road.

Beyond the lake, a Qashqai encampment straddled a small plateau with grazing of buff-coloured grass. Just beyond, in the foothills, was a small Qashqai village. The women were down among the reeds near an old stone bridge, gathering water from the trickle of a spring into black sheepskins. The legs were sealed with string and when the bag was full, the neck was turned and

tied. Their work was systematic and they took care not to muddy
the water until all the bags were bulging. Then placing one on each
hip, the women swung their way home.

At the entrance to the village stood a miniature caravanserai,* its
arched portal shading a blind man and two children scratching in
the dust. As I passed, a woman came out with a leather bottle.

'Greetings, traveller,' she called. 'Please, refresh yourself with
water.'

'That's kind. I'm very thirsty.'

'Come and rest before you continue,' she said. And taking me by
the arm, she led me into the shade, placing some cushions for my
comfort. She went to a small recess in the opposite wall where two
hens were pecking, placed a kettle on the open fire, and from a mud
shelf, took a dented metal teapot. From a brown paper bag, she
carefully measured half a palmful of tea, and tucked the bag away
behind some rusty tins. She swilled out some glasses, made the tea
and brought them over to me.

'Would the children like some?' I asked.

'It's all for you,' she replied, smiling. Her face was broad, almost
circular in shape, with shining cheeks and rounded forehead. But it
was not fat: her nose was bony, her brows angled over tilting eyes,
and her chin jutted out beneath a wide mouth. She had tied a cream
silk scarf round her wiry hair, and her gold tabard hung limply over
a single skirt. She was a tall woman, her shoulders thrown back,
and when she sat, she used no support for her back. Her only
jewellery was a tin bangle.

'Welcome,' she said, giving me more tea. 'My name is Sakina.'

'And I'm called John.'

She looked at me closely. 'But you're a girl.'

I shook my head. 'No, no, I'm a boy. I'm only sixteen.'

'I sense you're a girl. Still, let's leave the matter alone, you'll tell
me when you want to.'

I wanted to, but I felt it would be unwise.

'I'm a boy,' I repeated. 'So is it all right to be here with you?'

'Yes, of course. I have no husband to be jealous. He died three
years ago.'

As we sat talking, a lorry drew up. Some men entered to greet
Sakina warmly and drink noisily the water she offered. After much

* Quadrangular inn, with enclosed courtyard.

banter, they left, dropping a few coins in the lap of the blind man, her father. He took out a handkerchief, and fumbling for the coins, put them in and tied a knot. Then he hid it in the breast of his shirt.

'That'll buy tomorrow's bread,' said Sakina, patting the old man's cheek.

She depended for food on the generosity of passers-by, but it seemed she would not starve, for under Islamic law they were generous.

'Charity is the third act of piety,' said Jesus Christ in Qum, 'for a man must spend his wealth in the service of God, first helping himself and his family, then others. And he must always help orphans and the poor.

'And to remove something harmful, that even is charity. For the Holy Quran uses many words for charity: spending wealth, doing good to others, truthfulness, making oneself clean. And one of the words, Zakat, is a voluntary tax for all practising Muslims—a fifth of a man's profit, which is distributed

'To the poor and the needy, and those
Employed to administer the funds;
Alms are for those whose hearts
Have been recently reconciled
to Truth; for those in bondage
And in debt; and the wayfarer,
    And for those whose
    Cause is God's.

'And a man's charity is rewarded accordingly. Take the man who refused a beggar some bread.

' "Well what about a bit of fat?" asked the beggar.

' "Fat? Do you take me for a butcher's shop?"

' "A pinch of flour then, sir?"

' "Certainly not. We're not a mill."

' "At least some water, sir."

' "We're not a river either. I haven't got anything to give you."

'At that, the beggar walked into the house and pulled down his trousers.

125

' "Hey!" cried the owner. "What are you doing?"

' "Well, sir, since this place is such a desert, there's nothing else but to relieve myself." '

Later that afternoon, Sakina turned to me.

'Will you stay here as my guest? It's not very comfortable, but we'd look after you with care.'

'I'd love to, but the rest house in Kazerun is expecting me back, and they might get anxious.'

'Then you must go. But will you come again another day?'

'Tomorrow?'

'We'd be honoured.'

The next morning I arrived to find Sakina sweeping the court-yard with a loose bunch of twigs. She looked startled when I went in.

'But I thought you were coming tomorrow.'

'Oh? Is it difficult? Shall I go away?'

'No, please stay. It's just, being Friday, I can't buy meat. I was going to prepare something special.'

She hurried out to the village, leaving me to play with the children. She came back with the bottom of her tabard pulled up into a bulging pouch, which she emptied at my feet. A pile of aubergines fell into the dust and, picking them up and wiping them, she gave me several to munch.

We sat in the shade as a flow of people passed. The gendarme came first to make sure I really wanted to be there; then men on their way to the fields, inquisitive children, and women spinning wool into balls of yarn. They sat with us gossiping, the women and men mixing freely, and both looking after the children.

We ate lunch of an egg whipped into tomatoes and aubergines, and I gave Sakina some turkish delight from Kazerun: there is a Persian custom that a person brings home the speciality of the place he has visited—nougat from Isfahan, baklava from Yezd, *sohan* from Qum. She was delighted, and opened the box immediately, letting her children take as many pieces as they could hold.

After lunch, Sakina made me rest in a windowless room filled with tools, pots, bedding, and a sack of wheat. Later, she opened some boxes and showed me her treasures of worn brocade, beads, biro-pens, a plastic flower and some yellowing photographs. And when I gave her children a cotton neckscarf and a pair of plastic goggles—items for Mephistopheles—she immediately locked them away with the rest.

I spent several days there, mainly sitting, drinking tea, collecting water and visiting people in the village. The blind man seldom spoke and the children sat quietly in a corner of the courtyard. Their only toy was a broken top, and when I drew pin-men, or ran three-legged races, they laughed and asked for more. Fatima, the daughter, was eleven, with small gold earrings pierced through her lobes. She was skinny, with a cylindrical nose and thumb-sucking teeth. The boy's head was shaved to prevent the nesting of bugs; he looked frail, loved jokes, and impishly tickled Fatima's feet.

Sitting with the same people, I became aware of the sensitivity between them. With a slight movement of the hand, or a flicker of the eyes, they communicated a thought or courtesy which was returned by similar movement, and they seemed intuitively to know I was a girl; those with whom I had sat for some time insisted I was a girl; those who had seen me a short while thought I was a boy. My last evening, as I was settling down to sleep, Sakina and Fatima came into the room.

'We're sad you're leaving,' said Sakina.

'I'm sad too. I could stay here for days.'

'Before you go, will you tell us yourself you're a girl?'

'Yes, Sakina, I'm a girl.'

'Will you prove it?'

I lifted my shirt and girdle to reveal my breasts. She clapped her hands and chuckled.

'I knew we were the same.' And she hugged me affectionately.

The next day, I headed back for Kazerun. It was afternoon and I was thinking how much I would like to sleep when suddenly Mephistopheles choked and began to lose speed. I tried to accelerate, but he only went slower. He choked again, and stopped completely. I got off, cursing; I examined the petrol tank, but it was half-full. I examined the sparking plug but it seemed quite secure. I did not know what else to do, and as I had no desire to walk several miles to Kazerun in such heat, I sat down and slept. I woke two hours later and was about to start walking when I saw a man on a motor-bike coming towards me.

'Anything wrong?' he asked, as he passed.

'Yes, I've broken down.'

He got off and ambled towards Mephistopheles. He was bow-legged, with large flat feet. He could not find the cause, so pulled out a rubber coil and lashed it round the handlebars.

'I'll give you a tow.'

Each time he slowed for a bump, the rubber coil slackened and I had to brake; but then he accelerated and it tightened, only to stretch so that I had to brake again. I felt like an uncontrolled yo-yo.

When we reached Kazerun, the streets were full of people out for an evening stroll. When the younger men saw us, they began to cheer, and ran alongside, holding on to my bike, patting my back, and twanging the rubber coil.

I left Mephistopheles with a mechanic, but when I returned, the engine was still dismantled. The man looked up despairingly.

'Where did you get this bike?'

'In Isfahan.'

'The dogs. It's a terrible bike.'

'But what's wrong?'

'There was sand in the petrol tank. But all the engine is nearly worn through.'

I squatted on the floor beside him.

'Is it my fault?' I asked with concern. 'I've only had it a few weeks.'

'Oh no, the damage is years old. I doubt if you'll get back to Isfahan.'

I did not know whether to believe him, but somewhat cowardly decided to return by bus and hand back Mephistopheles. Poor thing, he had certainly lived up to his name, and though I had no desire to lose him, I felt I could no longer cope with him. It would mean a return to travelling by bus, which saddened me. On a bike, it was easier to explore remote areas and to stop as I wished. The terrain passed slowly, to be studied, remembered, and the challenge of hills, heat and dust made the journey more rewarding. Above all, I felt Mephistopheles enabled me to participate more than spectate, and he was a valuable accomplice in proving my masculinity.

I was also disconsolate at leaving the south, for I had felt a sense of peace and harmony there. Perhaps it was only the high mountains, which seemed to give Fars a rarefied atmosphere, cut off from the cosmopolitan north. But probably it was the people themselves who as tribesmen were more independent, and as nomads appealed to my own feelings for movement and mountains.

When I reached Isfahan, I bought some earrings to send to Sakina. A friend agreed to write a letter in Persian, which I outlined in English.

'Could you say I'm very grateful for all her hospitality, and that I value her friendship. Then say I'm enclosing a small present in thanks.'

The letter came out like this:

> To the Gracious Presence of my Dearest and
> Kindest of all Friends,
>
> May you always be in the possession of the
> gift of health and the heavenly treasure of
> happiness. Your favour was great and your
> generosity worth more than Khusrau's gold.
> In my humbleness, I offer you a gift in no
> way worthy of your bounteous self. Compared
> to your kindness, it is below nothing, a green
> leaf from a dervish, but to follow the saying:
>
> > O! Dearest! It is the habit of
> > the ants to offer as a gift a
> > locust's leg to King
> > Solomon.
>
> May this gift act as a token of remembrance,
> and may my eyes be brightened again with the
> sight of your person. May the peace of
> God fill your days with joy and wisdom.

7   *Women for Sale?*

BY CHANCE a week later at nine o'clock in the morning I was standing outside a house among a large crowd. Many of the people had slanting eyes, their short lashes partly concealed by overhanging lids; their nostrils were almost vertical, like those of a pekinese.

The men were dressed in grey frock coats, and black woolly hats shaped like Nefertiti's crown. The women wore long robes over baggy trousers which clutched the ankle in an embroidered band, and over their heads were shawls patterned with scarlet roses. Young boys, in tatty shirts and trousers, pushed their way through the crowd, yelling in high-pitched voices.

Suddenly a young man and his parents emerged from the house, and the women began a piercing wail, and the men to grunt and throw their hats in the air. The three people climbed into the wedding car—a pale blue American Ford, with high fin tails and deep chrome bumpers. A new carpet covered the roof, and from the bonnet sprouted plastic roses, white voile and ribbons. It led the other cars with reasonable dignity, their radios blaring, their aerials waving with nylon scarves. Then the procession reached a roundabout and the drivers went berserk. They skimmed round once like bumper cars, and continued to go round again, with their male passengers leaning out, brandishing their hats and yelling. Those who were more timid turned into the main street again, swerving from side to side. The bridal car itself gathered considerable speed down the straight, but frequently had to brake as a car overtook and cut in. Even when the cars reached the end of the town where the road was a pot-holed track, they continued equally fast, and the passengers clutched each other whenever the car hit a bump.

Outside the town near a river, we halted, the cars scattered across the road. The bridegroom and his parents went into the bride's house, and as the crowd settled into groups, I found myself with five young men.

Women for Sale?

'What's she like, Ahmad?' asked one.

'How should I know? I've never seen her.'

'Oh, come, you boasted you'd walked down the street with her, the whole of one afternoon.'

'So I did,' said Ahmad defensively, but admitted: 'Her father was walking between us.'

'Sucking up to him, were you?'

Ahmad lunged out.

'Shut up, you two,' said another. 'She's beyond your pocket. They say she's costing ten thousand *toman*. Don't you know how rich Mohammad's parents are?'

Ahmad stood still and whistled, passing a hand over the top of his head.

'Ten thousand?' He clenched his arm to swell his biceps and felt it with his left hand. He frowned. 'There's a car for sale at the garage for only eight thousand.'

'But it wouldn't last so long. I'd rather have a wife than a car after fifteen years—*and* she'd make money for me.'

'Well, I'm going to America,' said another. 'I'll get a wife there, without paying a thing.'

I was in Gunbad-i-Qabus, the centre of the Yomut and Goklan Turkmen tribes, where I had arrived the preceding day by bus. We had passed through the Elburz mountains, whose blue fingers of hills gripped the edge of a plateau and rose into peaks like knuckles. Then we descended gradually into greenness, first with bushes and scrub vegetation, then oak and sycamore trees. Paddy-fields dropped in terraces down the valley, and striped expanses of corn and cotton covered the lower slopes. Ahead, moving northwards, the plain was speckled with grass, translating the Caspian belt into Central Asian steppe—the home of the Turkmen tribe.

For me, the Turkmen presented another facet of Persia, for though by nationality Iranian, they are a tribe with a different cultural heritage. True, such heritage might seem barbaric, for they come from the Mongols and Turks who swarmed across Asia into Central Anatolia and back. But they also come from the Mongols who invaded, and gave so much impetus to Persia in the thirteenth and fourteenth centuries.

However the renown of the Turkmen comes more from the nineteenth century, when they lawlessly controlled the regions east of the Caspian. They sallied, they pillaged, they raped; they attacked pilgrims and travellers who were trying to reach Samarqand and Bokhara; and they constantly raided caravans.

Their cruelty seemed limitless. In the 1920's, the Turkmen cut off the heads of their Persian enemies and stuffed the skins with straw, to display on their tents as trophies. But the period as a whole seems vicious, for in return the skins of Turkmen heads were sent to the Shah as gifts.

Now the Turkmen are subjugated, their tribe divided immutably between Russian and Iranian territory. And those who remained in Iran have settled, still east of the Caspian, to cultivate one of the country's more fertile areas. But they still retain the tradition of making their Turkmen carpets, and they still follow the Sunni branch of Islam.

Inside the bride's house, negotiations continued; a contract was signed, and cash payment made for the bride. Then two men brought out a dressing-table. They heaved it onto the roof of the bridal car and strapped it down with a rope. They went back to the house and re-emerged with a bulging saddle-bag, a branching clothes-stand, and a sheep. They dropped them into the boot, and then Mohammad, his parents and the bride's parents climbed into the car. The bride followed meekly, in a white shawl printed with flowers, and was squashed unceremoniously between her parents. I caught a glimpse of her greasy complexion, but was not to see her again throughout the celebrations.

The procession of cars returned with equal enthusiasm to the bridegroom's house, and the women were ushered in. The iron gates were closed, and Mohammad and his friends climbed onto the wall above the street. Ahmad saw me among the crowd.

'Mister John,' he yelled. 'Get in, GET INSIDE.'

They hurled empty tins and chips of wood to the crowd, and often the smallest boys, when men were fighting above them, searched low on the ground and found them. Punching their way to the wall, they handed them up to the thrower and received one *toman*. Then Mohammad took a bundle of notes, and screwing them up one by one, he tossed them into the crowd. The boys grew wild, and battled for the money; soon noses were bleeding, shirts were torn, and a few boys were settling old scores.

In an enclosed courtyard, away from the women, we wagered our money on wrestlers, and at one o'clock when it grew too hot, we started the wedding lunch. The women brought in huge platters of food, and when we had finished, we moved to the shade while they cleared away.

'Come and sit with us, Mister,' said one boy called Meshed. He was dressed in a brown tweed suit, and beads of sweat trickled down his forehead which he kept wiping with a large handkerchief. His shoulders were pulled forward by the tightness of his jacket, for he was fat, and his face was so puffy that his cheeks seemed to sweep straight into his eyelids, with only a slanting gap for his eyes.

'Welcome to the wedding,' he said. 'Welcome to the wedding.' And he pushed a boy away so that I could sit beside him.

'You like our wedding?' he asked. 'You must come to mine.'

'Congratulations. When are you getting married?'

'He can't afford a wife yet,' said another, 'but he thinks he'll have the prettiest girl in Gunbad.' He picked up a pebble and threw it at the back of a boy's head some ten yards away, just missing.

'Who?' asked Meshed. 'You mean that cotton-grower's daughter? She's no good. She can't even cook.'

The boy took hold of Meshed's arm, pinching it hard.

'Do you speak about my cousin like that? Do you? Do you?' And he twisted Meshed's arm till he was writhing on the ground. 'She's a good cook, and she can milk, and she can weave, *and* she's got big breasts. What else do you want in a woman?' And he spat in Meshed's face.

'Marriage is a sacred thing,' said Jesus Christ in Qum, 'and no-one should marry against their wishes. Our Holy Prophet, peace be upon Him, allowed a girl to divorce, for her father had forced her to marry a man she did not like.

'Now both may decide the terms of contract,
their house, their servants, her welfare;
and the man must pay her a dowry
to allow her some independence.

'Such is the law for all Muslims, but the Shi'as have *mut'a* as well. That is, a couple may sign a contract of marriage for only a specific period. Then they are free, but if any children result, they are both responsible for the rest of their lives. You see, *mut'a* prevents shame and sin, and we have no such thing as illegitimate children.'

'But doesn't it lead to prostitution?' I asked.

'Yes, sometimes, but those are people who don't understand. And how many women will enter into a day's contract just to satisfy a man?'

'And there's no divorce at the end?'

'No, though divorce exists for longer contracts.

> 'Divorce is allowed but not recommended,
> for what humans are perfect partners?
> Now both man and woman may call for divorce,
> But the man is specially commanded
> to make provision for his former wife—
> *the affluent man according to his means,*
> *and according to his means the needy man*
> *honourably.**

'And I suppose you'll bring up polygamy?' said Jesus Christ, just as I was about to ask him. 'But can you say Europeans are monogamous with their divorces and passing lovers? Indeed, there are practical reasons for having more than one wife:

> '*If you fear that you will not act justly*
> *towards the orphans, marry such women*
> *as seem good to you, two, three, four;*
> *but if you fear you will not be equitable*
> *then only one . . .†*

'Yet at the same time, in the same *sura*, the Holy Quran comments:

> '*You will not be able to be equitable*
> *between your wives, be you ever so eager.‡*

* Quran, 2 'The Cow'.   † Quran, 4 'Women'.
‡ Quran, 4, 'Women'.

134

Women for Sale?

Meshed picked himself sheepishly off the ground.

'Come on, Mister,' he said, 'I'm going to show you the sights of Gunbad.'

We walked into the main street and Meshed leant against a doorway.

'There are beautiful girls in Gunbad,' he said, pointing to one whose nose was squashed like a boxer's. 'Did you see her breasts?' And his face flushed with excitement.

'Mm, not bad,' I said, laughing.

Another girl passed, her face covered with spots. Meshed nudged me. 'Look at those hips. Beautiful. I'd never get my arms round.'

We moved on, but stopped to have our shoes cleaned so that we could watch a group of girls nearby.

She's pretty, I thought, with those peaceful eyes. Firm arms too —she'd hold a man or a child well. I pointed her out to Meshed.

'But you can't like her, she's far too thin. What about that one on the right? I bet she costs a lot. I always pick the most expensive.'

'Well, if money didn't matter, what sort of a woman would you choose?'

'Oh, she'd have to be beautiful, and . . . and . . .' He seemed unable to express his physical desires. 'Of course she'd cook well, and give me lots of children. And she mustn't argue, and she must love me, and do what I tell her, oh and lots more.'

I thought how differently the Persians spoke of their women, though it was true that in action I had experienced discrimination in Isfahan. But they seemed to speak, and to think, more of the ideal of women, like the ideal of gardens. In literature especially, as in French medieval literature, the woman is elevated to a symbol of purity, exquisite beauty and chastity; or else she is thought of as the wine of sensuality. But either way, a man is moved to ecstasy.

'Well, mister,' said Meshed, jauntily. 'What sort of wife would you want?'

'I don't mind about her body,' I said condescendingly, 'though I'd like her to have soft skin. She'd be kind, and imaginative, and definitely independent. And we'd bring up the children together.'

Meshed looked puzzled, and kicked at a stone. And I could not work out myself whether I had been speaking as a man, or a woman, or just as a European.

We went into a tea-house, and Meshed ordered a large bowl of meat and rice, but the pursuit of girls had not raised my appetite beyond a glass of tea. To my left was an old man sitting alone at a table, his woolly Turkmen hat on his lap. A scar ran from the side of his nose to his left ear, and the top of one thumb was missing.

Over to the right was a non-Turkmen family. The mother thrust breadcrumbs in a baby's mouth, the father smoked, and two boys rolled glasses across the table. A girl of about fourteen drank coca-cola, and as she leant forward, her veil fell open. She caught my eye, and I smiled. She smiled back. I lowered my stare to her blouse, and looking down too, she flushed and pulled her veil hastily round her. Then, slowly, she looked at me again. I rested my chin on my hand and partly in joke, partly in seriousness, I pouted my mouth. She flushed again, but did the same. Suddenly her mother slapped her across the arm, and the girl jumped round, to sit with her back to me. But when the family was leaving, the girl glanced at me. As she got up, she carefully revealed a bare calf, and as she passed, she brushed my extended feet with her veil.

The following morning we went to the bridegroom's house for more celebrations. There was little to do except gorge oneself, wrestle or talk about women and money, so I slipped away for the afternoon to wander round the town. The houses were rectangular, two-storey blocks, with sloping tent-roofs, drainpipes and windows. They were not secret, not private, and showed more the influence of Russian domestic architecture than Persian mud dwellings.

In one shop, some antique saddle-bags hung on a wall, their bases thick with large tassels in reds and deep orange. The body of one bag zigzagged with lines which juddered like a micro-wave. Another had horizontal diamonds, its edges picked out in orange. But the backgrounds of both were deep mulberry, a traditional colour of the Yomut Turkmen.

Beneath was a pile of carpets which had recently been made in Gunbad; and all had the traditional Turkmen *gul*, a stylised flower in the shape of a polygon and sectioned into four. In each one, the *gul* marched across the carpet in a series of orderly lines, and I immediately liked the solidity which such geometry effected. But as I looked at one, then at an identical second and third, I began to grow less interested and to wish for more variety. The colours however provided plenty of variation—not the traditional rusty browns and soft reds, but scarlet mingled with citrine yellow, bright blue and white, or a dazzling lime bordered by palest turquoise.

In the next shop, I found some magnificent Turkmen jewellery. Bands of silver for the wrist, six inches wide and an eighth thick, had lines of oval cornelians set in parallel troughs. There was a spade-shaped pendant, weighing two pounds, whose surface was damascened with arabesques of gold; a belt, whose leather was studded with hundreds of silver teeth; and delicate prayer-holders, embossed with bold patterns. The shapes were simple, but imposing, and reminded me of Celtic jewellery.

I was surprised, for I had no idea the Turkmen produced such beautiful work. Maybe I was unjust to be surprised, but the symmetry and rhythm seemed alien to their former rapacity. For all of this jewellery was antique, and had been sold by the Turkmen to dealers for cash when, subjugated, they were no longer able to plunder.

Once, the Turkmen women had worn a great weight of silver daily, even when they worked; but now I had noticed that few of them wore jewellery, perhaps only a bangle or cheap earrings. And in the shops there were many examples of modern work. Light-weight pendants, silver-plated earrings set with coloured glass, and charms and baubles on narrow tin collars instead of coins and prayer-holders. True, some of the traditional designs were used, but they seemed flimsy counterparts which lacked the skill of craftsmanship and had lost the sense of harmony.

That evening, we gathered again in Mohammad's house, for he was still separated from his bride, and he sat in the corner drinking tea, letting his friends entertain him. They moved in a circle, thrusting their pelvises out at each other, and jumping up and down. Then one boy went to the centre and pretended to wrestle, his thick arms grasping his head.

I had scarcely met the bridegroom, for he was constantly surrounded by friends. Indeed I found it hard to distinguish between them all, both with characters and features. They had an ebullience which over-rode any sense of decorum, and they laughed loudly each time a joke was repeated. Apart from their Mongoloid features, none of them had beards by which I could distinguish them—the Turkmen are known for their hairlessness, and I felt for a change quite proud of my own hairless chin.

After supper, one of the boys called out:

'Come on, we'd better leave him to it.' And making lewd gestures, everyone jostled out. There was to be a private ceremony, with a mulla and witnesses, and then for the first time, Mohammad would be left with his bride.

We paraded down the street like schoolboys, playing pebble-football, and singing as loudly as we could. One boy began to run, shouting:

'I'm beating you, I'm beating you to the end of the street.'

Everyone started to run, their chests out, their shoulders held tightly back. But I could not compete, for I would certainly reveal a chest which swung; so when the others stopped and turned to see where I was, I let out a howl and yelled:

'Ayeee, a bear's just bitten my leg.' And clutching my thigh, I staggered forward crying, 'Look out, look out, it's coming your way.' Several leapt forward and with imaginary guns, blasted the poor bear off the road.

Such physical games were exacting, for each time I had to provide an excuse. First there was wrestling, which I could not do since I had 'recently broken an arm'. That also excused me from weight-lifting; and finally I said I played only cricket, 'an English game which you don't play?' 'No,' came the answer, 'but let's see who throws stones furthest.'

But apart from these tests, I no longer felt concerned about my disguise; indeed I sometimes felt the disguise had taken over, that I really was a boy. 'The mask was apparently beginning to walk on its own and to ignore my plans. I didn't consider this particularly bothersome, but it was nevertheless strange.'* Quite unconsciously, I would size up the shape of a woman's legs, or speculate, with the other boys, what important jobs we would soon secure as men. Was my character beginning insidiously to change, or was it only the effect of the Turkmen boys I was with who were convinced of

* Kobo Abé, *The Face of Another* (trs. E. Dale Saunders), London 1969.

their own superiority—so that only occasionally I remembered to protest?

We went to Gunbad's only monument, a buttressed cylinder topped by a dunce's cap in brick, which stretches phallicly 150 feet from a bare earth mound. There is no staircase either inside or out, and only one small window in the roof facing east. It was built in 1006 as a tomb tower for Qabus,* and his glass coffin was probably suspended at the top of the tower.

We walked round the vast base of the building and someone lit a cigarette which was passed to us all to puff. We played noughts-and-crosses in the dust, conquered Russia with sub-machine guns, and then took Turkey and Europe. We were equipping ourselves against the States when Meshed said petulantly:

'Well, *I'm* not going to fight—I'm going to study there.'

'You'll only get there if *we're* ruling,' said our commander, and the invasion began.

On our way home, we met two of the wedding guests.

'Hello,' said Jimmy, who had been in England and wore trousers from Carnaby Street with a pink silk shirt. 'Do you want to come home? You can't possibly want to go to that dreadful wedding again.'

We went to his uncle's house where he gave me a deck-chair to sit in.

'My uncle's a famous archaeologist,' said Jimmy. 'Do you want to see his slides?'

I nodded.

'This is the Arc de Triomphe,' he said, and went on to show me Nelson's Column, the hotel at Ealing, and Bond Street.

'London's fantastic,' he said. 'And all those girls. So *free*.'

'Yes, I suppose they do what they want.'

'They certainly do. They absolutely fell for me.' And he arched his back, closing his eyes.

His uncle picked up a violin. The joints of his fingers were large, the skin smooth and creamy, so that his hands resembled chicken-bones. But when he began to play, they moved supply along the strings. He began with a classical Persian sequence, and announced each type in turn: *Mahur, Shur, Dashti*. And as he played, I felt

---

* Dailami king of the Ziyarids, ruling the Caspian provinces of Gurgan and Tabaristan. He died in A.D. 1012.

the same serenity, the same absorption as when I had sat tracing the patterns of a mosaic faience. It seemed as though music were related to other Persian arts, with their intricate detail and repetition. There were no sudden bursts or jumps, but being monophonic, it developed steadily, exploring and repeating small intervals, and always returning to certain dominant notes. Showy brilliance was not its theme: it was more intimate, more mystical, with every note embroidered. For 'a note without ornament is like a night without the moon, a river without water, a flower without perfume, a loved woman without jewels.'*

'Stupid all these boys in Gunbad,' said Jimmy suddenly, 'They're so narrow-minded. Can only think about their wretched women. What do *they* know about women?' And he closed his eyes again.

The old man moved on to folk dances and tribal songs. They were rhythmic and strongly melodic, and reminded me now of Scottish music, now of gypsy music in France. Indeed it is arguable that Western gypsy music originated partly in Persian music. A group of musicians and blacksmiths, called 'loree', moved from the Indus Valley to the Sassanian court, when Bahram Gur married a Sindhi princess. Firdausi mentions 'ten thousand selected male and female *loriyan* musicians'.† Then they moved west with Islam, and took with them their music, now combined with Persia's. And as they passed, groups dropped off in Turkey and Europe, North Africa and Spain—to become the gitano, tsigane, romany, who still have their musicians and blacksmiths.

There was still one more day of celebrations, the 'farewell party', but when we went to Mohammad's house, we were not allowed to see his bride. His friends seemed more subdued and showed a new respect for this boy who had at last experienced a woman.

We sat against the walls, toasting his health and joy in tea. And as was the custom, Mohammad replied:

'Now we'll see who's got strong stomachs. Those who don't finish a full pot of tea must forfeit ten *toman*.'

They were large pots, and I already felt saturated; but as I was

* Alain Daniélou, *Inde du Nord*, Paris 1966.
† Quoted in A. Balouch, *Spanish Cante Jondo and its origin in Sindhi Music*, Hyderabad 1968.

short of money, I decided I must not lose. I drank off a bowlful and
poured out another to cool; I drank the second and third, but
when it came to the fourth, I could feel the liquid against my
stomach. I looked at the others. A few were belching or sagging
their heads. I drank down the fifth and the sixth, and noted that
only two people were drinking still. I drained the teapot with the
next bowlful and then sat back, breathing heavily, and congratu-
lating myself that I was not to forfeit my money. But though the
losers were booed, I noticed with resentment that not one of them
paid their fine.

'And now,' said Mohammad, 'we'll bet on our ambitions. You,
Ahmad, you start.'

'All right,' he said. 'I'll bet four hundred *toman* I've got a car
when I'm twenty-two.'

'That's not fair,' shouted everyone. 'You know your father's
giving you one.'

'I'll bet,' squeaked another boy. 'Twenty *toman* I shall have a
cottonfield.'

'What's twenty *toman*?' bawled everyone.

'Well I,' said another, 'will be Tehran's best doctor. And then
you'll have to pay to see me.'

'And m-me,' said Meshed, shaking with excitement. He stood
up. 'Fifty thousand *toman* that I'll get to America.'

'Done,' yelled everyone with glee.

Then Mohammad left the room and returned with an armful
of scarves, which he handed out to his friends: turquoise nylon,
pink gauze, green dacron, scarlet cotton. And to me, he gave a
Turkmen shawl of silk, patterned in crocus yellow on a black background.

'This is for *your* bride,' he laughed. 'She must wear it at her
wedding.'

The other boys clustered round to look at it and finger it.

'Mister John, try it on,' shouted Meshed.

'I don't want to look like a girl.'

'Go on, it might suit you.' And he draped it over my head. I
contorted my face into a hideous expression so that all femininity
would be disguised.

'Doesn't she look beautiful? Oh, I want you for my wife. Please
come over here and show us.'

I stood up and mimicked a woman, mincing my steps, blinking my eyelids and jerking my hips unrhythmically. Then I pulled off the shawl and strode back to where I had been sitting.

The acclamations were loud. 'Well done, Mister John. Hooray. Well acted. Give us more. We love you.'

Perhaps unfairly I felt I had seen enough, for the Turkmen could be monotonous, rather like their carpets. Giving my dictionary to Mohammad and a book to Meshed, I left that afternoon for Gurgan, a town some sixty miles away which once had been the base of the Qajar dynasty, and a stronghold against the Turkmen. But the inhabitants then seemed no better than their enemies, for 'one of them had enticed an aged uncle into the desert, and there sold him for eight kurrauns to a Toorcoman . . . the Khan had heard of this, and by good luck managed to seize both the buyer and seller . . . he proposed, on the morrow, to boil the [seller] in a cauldron, and then kill the Toorcoman, having first made him breakfast on a boiled leg of the nephew!'*

Now Gurgan has an air of modernity, with its avenues, banks, and a cinema. But as I found mainly farm equipment to look at, I took a bus to Pahlevi Dez where the Turkmen hold a market of their products, from carpets and hats, to shovels and horses. We drove over a corrugated track between hedges of rushes and myrtle, crossed the deeply-gorged Gurgan river by a single-track humped bridge, and arrived in the village. Two streets led at right angles from each other and petered out on the plain; three shops had few goods and no customers. Everything seemed dirty and depressed: the houses had rotting balconies and shutters, rusted roofs and drainpipes; the earth, a grey-tinged sienna, was baked into grooves after winter rains.

An aspiring linguist called 'Umar offered to show me the local crafts: carpets knotted in dark rooms; bread baked in ovens sunk into the street; and felt, where strands of wool were applied in scrolls to half-compacted wool.

'I'll take you to see some Turkmen tents tomorrow,' he said, as it grew dark. 'And you can stay with me.'

His home was a tiny hut about ten feet square. He flung his jacket on the ground and stretched out on the rug.

* W. R. Holmes, *Sketches on the Shores of the Caspian*, London 1845.

'Horribly small, isn't it? But my father's building a huge house right next door.'

His father arrived, a white-haired man, half-blind. He lit a candle and laid some bread and cheese on the floor.

'My mother's dead,' commented 'Umar, not helping.

'I'm sorry.'

'Yes, so I'm really the head of the family.' He rubbed the pile of the carpet. 'It's very old, this rug.'

'I can see. It's beautiful.'

'Yes. A professor wanted to buy it, but I said no. Of course you can have it, for a thousand *toman*.'

'I'm very honoured, but . . .'

'All right, nine hundred.'

He reduced the price to five hundred before he realised I would not buy it.

Towards eleven o'clock, someone rapped on the door. 'Umar opened it and called me to come.

'The gendarme's here. He wants you to go and have your passport checked.'

'Oh, of course. I should have done it before.'

We walked into the street, and the gendarme peered at me.

'What's his name?' he asked 'Umar.

'John. He's from England.'

'Football in England is good, Mr. John?'

'Oh yes, I play twice a week.'

'Do you play for England?'

In the gendarmerie, we went to the office.

'Good evening,' said the man behind the desk. 'Your passport please. Only a routine check.'

I unzipped my pocket, and he asked: 'You like our little town, sir?'

'I haven't been here long, you know.'

'Yes, I know.'

I handed him the passport and started to laugh. He came to the photograph and laughed as well, pointing to the photograph and then at me. 'Umar went to look.

'This is really you?'

'Yes, and nobody guessed.'

'No, nobody,' laughed the officer, slapping his thigh in delight.

143

Then suddenly his face snapped into anger. 'Why didn't you report here before? The Russian border is only fifty kilometres. And why are you here?'

'But—'

'You must be a Russian spy,' he shouted. 'You filthy boy, I shall have to arrest you.'

'Arrest me? No, no I'm not a Russian spy.'

'You must be, else why would you wear a disguise? I must arrest you and send you to Gurgan tomorrow.' He stood up, his face tightening with emotion. 'They'll send you to Tehran, and there' —he leaned forward, glaring with contempt—'you'll be thrown into prison.'

At the sound of his shouting, a gendarme rushed in. The officer pointed at me and hissed: 'Russian spy.'

I stood up and said, with control: 'I . . . am . . . not . . . a Russian spy. Look,' and I snatched the passport from his desk. 'Look, it says here "British Passport".'

'This man is a Russian spy,' he bawled at the others.

'I AM NOT A MAN.' Then, more quietly: 'Do Russians write in English?' and I pulled out my diaries and books. This made the officer think for a moment before he resumed his accusations.

For some reason, 'Umar took my side and tried to pacify the officer, who eventually left the room to discuss with the other gendarmes. Alone with me, 'Umar pushed himself against me, trying to kiss me and put his hand down the front of my shirt. I thrust him away.

'But you're a woman. So beautiful,' he murmured. 'Just let me touch you,' and his hand slid up my thigh. I hit his arm hard and crossed the room where I leant against the wall, my legs crossed and my arms protecting my chest. He followed me.

'Aaah, tonight, what joy we can have. And you can have my carpet.' He assumed a nonchalant air. 'I know influential people— *they* wouldn't let you go to prison.'

The officer returned and the argument started again, until finally I burst into tears. He looked puzzled.

'Well is she just a woman then?' he asked, and after some consideration, began to take down my passport details.

'It's all right, now,' he said. 'We won't do anything. You can go home with 'Umar now.'

Women for Sale?

I did not relish the idea, so asked: 'Couldn't I sleep here? I mean, now that I'm a girl, it's a bit difficult.'

'Certainly, certainly, we have a roomful of bunks.' He pointed to one of the gendarmes. 'You. Show her where they are.'

I found some sheets on my bunk, and folding them round me I started to fall asleep. The door opened, and 'Umar crept in, feeling his way towards my bunk.

'I'd never harm you,' he whispered. 'I just want to kiss you.'

'Well I don't want to kiss you. Please go away,' and after a struggle he went to lie on the bunk beside mine.

The door opened again, and a gendarme sprang onto the bunk above 'Umar. Then the officer came in with another gendarme and they lay down to my left. There was silence. Then:

'I'll give you a hundred *toman*,' said the officer.

The soldier on the top bunk leant over, swinging a tin pendant which hung round his neck.

'Real silver,' he said. 'A hundred *toman* and this.'

'I'm not interested.'

'One hundred and fifty,' said a third voice, threateningly.

'I tell you I'm not interested.'

'Umar intervened. 'Don't you need the money?'

'I've got a thousand *toman* in Tehran.'

'Oh.'

Silence.

'I'll give you three hundred, now,' said the officer.

'Three fifty.'

'Four hundred.'

The bidding finally reached twenty-five pounds, but I could not determine if it was a joint offer, and any enquiry, I felt, might compromise me.

By now I was sitting up angrily, and extremely frightened, clutching the flimsy sheet round me. 'Umar came over once more to persuade me to accept the offer. I drew a knife from my pocket, though it was only a rusty penknife which would not have cut a melon rind. Someone whispered to my left.

'The officer says you can go to his house if you'd prefer privacy with him,' explained 'Umar.

'I prefer nothing. And tell that . . . that officer that when I get to Tehran, I'll report him to the head of the Military Police.'

Immediately the officer began to apologise. 'We thought you'd want to,' he said. 'I mean most European girls do that *we've* met.'

Soon I heard three people snoring, but 'Umar tiptoed across to my bunk. 'I've got a very rich friend in Gurgan. He likes English women. He'll give you five hundred *toman—and* a carpet of your own choice.'

After a few hours' uneasy sleep, I got up at five o'clock and went to fetch my bag from 'Umar's house. Near one of the shops we saw an old man leaning against a wall. 'Umar ran forward.

'Father,' he cried. 'What's the matter?'

'In the night. A pain. Here.' He tapped his heart. 'I'm dying,' and he raised his eyes to heaven. 'I waited for you, and waited. Oh, the pain.' And he hit his head again and again against the wall.

'Run,' said 'Umar, taking hold of my hand, and we raced to his home. He hurriedly changed his shirt, at the same time trying to kiss me. Then we banged on the door of a neighbouring house, and a man in pyjamas came sleepily out. We begged him to drive us to Gurgan, and he started an old Austin Cambridge, while 'Umar pushed me onto the front seat, climbing in beside me. We stopped for the old man who stretched himself on the back seat, panting, and the car went over the bridge, moving slowly towards Gurgan.

'She's nearly twenty years old,' said the driver proudly, patting the steering wheel.

'*Jan*,' gasped the old man behind us, each time we went over a bump. 'Ah, *jan*, life.'

'*Jan*,' whispered 'Umar into my ear. 'Darling, we can go and see my rich friend while my father's at the doctor.'

We parked in the main street of Gurgan, and supported the old man to the doctor's house. He was given an injection and a prescription, and by the time we returned to the car, he had stopped his heavy breathing. 'Umar went to buy the pills, and rather than face further assaults, I left the old man and ran to the nearest bus station to go back to Tehran.

I slept most of the way, but woke intermittently to look at the passing countryside. On the right was the Caspian, grey and lifeless, reminding me more of Bournemouth on an overcast day than the exotic breeding ground of sturgeon. On the left, like a wall

146

against the road, forest soared up the hills. Then came sorrel-coloured mountains with one snow-covered peak, for the land was changing itself to face the Iranian plateau.

I felt a sense of relief when we reached Tehran, for it seemed like security. But I was still confused about the Turkmen, for they had shown much hospitality and their jewellery was magnificent; yet at the same time they seemed to have a somewhat brutal disregard for human-beings. And it was strange, I thought, how when I was a boy I could fall in with their callousness, but the moment I was a girl, I felt humiliated and powerless.

8 *Quiescence*

HOPING TO TAKE away the taste of the Turkmen, I decided to go to the Valley of the Assassins, a place I had wanted to visit ever since a school lecture. I have never forgotten the photographs: great barren mountains protected tiny hamlets where fresh spring water irrigated beans and corn; small paths led to threshing tables where mules circled and men winnowed; and on open ground, women wove carpets on rickety looms, women who were dressed in tattered but brightly patterned petticoats and dresses. Above, on blocks of rock, were the remnants of castles, fortified places which dated back to the eleventh century.

But there was an air of intrigue as well, for these castles acted as a base for the Isma'ilis in their terrorist campaign against the orthodox Sunni. Basically the Isma'ilis were Shi'a, but they heretically claimed Isma'il as the Seventh Imam instead of his appointed younger brother. And although they virtually disappeared after the Mongol conquest, their name as Assassins persisted in Europe, and was perpetuated in legends and poetry. They were known as murderers, intriguers, anarchists, for the crusaders who brought back such tales had little understanding of their religious beliefs and motives.

I felt sufficiently confident to be in such a place, where there were no roads, no telephones, and few villages. Besides, these were the mountains where the legendary heroes of Iran had fought out their destinies, where Rustam had conquered the White Div, where Faridun sought refuge against the serpentine Zahhak.

I went to Qazvin and found a bus which would take me as far as Shahrak in the Elburz mountains. It was a dilapidated bus with broken windows, its roof piled precariously high with huge sacks, boxes and provisions, and the passengers were squashed into the seats, three to a place for two. It was the only bus for three days, and once on the road it stopped for anyone who flagged it down. By the time we started the long ascent into the mountains, the bus was packed, very hot, and smelling of paraffin, hens and people.

The road was single-tracked, twisting up the side in hairpin bends. Mostly the passengers shouted and sang, but whenever we approached a severe corner, they raised their voices louder, calling fervently on God. As the bus reversed to a precipitous edge, they sat nervously in silence. And the moment the bus got round, they thanked Allah joyously. We crawled upwards for nearly three hours, and reached the top of the pass above ten thousand feet.

Layer upon layer of hills hung like terracotta clouds beneath the sky. Their peaks swirled in a thick arc whose height was diminished by the weight of the sky. Their sides were gashed with ravines and waterless gullies, and their bases vied for space. Long ridges jutted down to the valley's river, like fingers grasping a strand of hair. The water threw flashes of white as it caught the sun, and its banks were green with trees and fields.

As we descended, I noticed more intimate details: a small hamlet tucked into a hollow, or a village at the head of a gorge; outcrops of rock which were rust in colour, and pitted like coral; a separate hump on which were the ruins of a fortress. Slowly the colour of the hills turned mauve, mixed with the blueness of evening shadow. Soon it was dark, and we stopped at an invisible village to offload some passengers. Several miles later we came to a slope of pebbles, piled up at the edges to define the road. At the bottom, the bus stopped and we all got out.

'Is this Shahrak?' I asked.

'No,' said the driver, gathering his belongings.

'But are you going further?' I asked.

'In a while.'

As far as I knew, he might mean several days, so I followed the others to the local *chai khane*. The proprietor was pouring tea from a cracked pot, and thumping lumps of sugar into blackened plastic bowls. A youth untied his bundle, and offered me some bread.

'Where are you going?' he asked.

'To Alamut,' I answered.

'Tonight?'

'Maybe, I don't know.' I had no idea what lay between Shahrak and Alamut.

'I shouldn't. Not at night.'

'Why not?'

He hunched his shoulders, and tightened his mouth. 'Evil spirits,' he whispered. 'They always kill foreigners.'

We both laughed. The skin of his face was like congealed fat as though it could not breathe; his curly hair was brushed back, except for a strand which waved on his forehead.

'I live at Alamut,' he said. 'I'll go straight home, and bring a mule in the morning for you.'

'But I'm quite happy walking,' I protested.

'It's no trouble. I charge twenty *toman*.'

The bus set off again and after an hour, we rounded a hill, to see the lights of Shahrak: we had taken over seven hours to go fifty miles. The passengers disappeared in the darkness, and I followed a path along the side of the hill. I could see only single lights flickering below, either from candles or paraffin lamps. The noise of water was somewhere beyond, and round me was the whirring of bats. I came to a dimly-lit tea-house, empty apart from moths, and I lay on one of the benches. They were covered with carpets which I soon discovered were full of fleas.

I woke early the next morning and got up to look outside. Some twenty-five house were spread over a slope whose lower perimeter was marked by trees. They were made of mud and wooden poles, and held a verandah in their sides. Each dwelling was protected by an encirclement of brushwood, and from some of the compounds, white smoke rose vertically, undisturbed by breeze.

I heard a clatter to the left and saw a youth and two mules threading between the houses.

'Salaam,' he called. 'I'm Araf's cousin. He told me to fetch you.'

His eyes were pinched from lack of sleep and from peering in the dark. He had a round, boyish face, and his skin was weathered brown so that his eyes stood out white.

'Did you find your way in the dark all right?' I asked.

He grinned. 'If a raven picked out my eyes, I could walk for six days in these hills and still know the ground.'

I jumped on one of the mules and we set off east down a pathway. Beyond the poplar trees which skirted the village was a wooden bridge with its planks missing, so we took the mules through the river, where a mist still hovered over boulder-shattered water. The hills were gold in the early sunlight—not tarnished gold, but pale from the chill of the air. Below, yellow rice-stubble sat in beds of cracked earth.

We followed a path hemmed in by stone walls and blackberry bushes which led to fields of wheat and beans, where men were beginning to work. We always kept near the river, near the walnut trees and willows, and after an hour, we stopped at a hamlet, whose houses balanced on stilts. Their bases were filled with hay, and some were walled in for cattle in winter. We climbed a ladder onto a roof where a woman was tossing rice on a tray, then picking it over. Wiping her forehead with her arm, she pointed to a room behind her, and said she would bring food.

There were no windows but I could see enough to swipe at the flies; Araf's cousin let them crawl over his face and hands. I kept looking at the doorway, for it framed a magnificent view: first a stack of straw, then the mottled leaves of trees, overlooked by hills which were heavily incised. As a backdrop, a higher range stood pale grey, touching the sheet of washed-out sky.

We crossed the river again, and headed northwards into the hills —rather I should say further into the hills for they already over-powered us. We passed a woman walking towards the river with an empty plastic bucket; we passed a flock of sheep going down to water; and then we were on a plateau, yellow with dead grass. The trees had died out, and the villages.

'Look, look,' said the boy. 'There's Alamut.' And he pointed to the hills ahead. I could see no ruins.

'At the top?' I asked.

'Are you an eagle? Look, there, at the bottom.'

A mound of solid rock was a footstool for the mountain. It was shaped like a tin jelly-mould, and stood separate from the other hills. As we drew closer, I could see a village at its base. There were water channels near it, cut in the side of a ravine we crossed. At the edge of the village was a threshing table, boxed in by a hedge which smelt of myrtle, and a man was leading a donkey round and round.

We dismounted in the village square, an open space abutted by houses. A stream trickled across one side next to three large walnut trees, which tradition claims were planted by Hasan-i-Sabbah, the Isma'ili leader who first occupied Alamut. He certainly built the water channels which helped Alamut to remain unconquered till it gave itself up to the Mongols. Once it was nearly captured, in 1118, after the surrounding crops had been destroyed by troops for eight successive years.

Araf appeared and told his cousin to water the mules and to take my bag to his house. He took me through the village, past the source of the stream where women were filling pots. We climbed steadily, and approached the fortress from behind, balancing along a knife edge. It was the only path of access, for elsewhere the sides dropped in vertical rock for several hundred feet—no wonder Hasan-i-Sabbah had chosen this place.

He was born in Qum in the mid-eleventh century and he moved to Rayy as a child. He was educated in the Shi'a tradition and says of himself: 'From the days of my boyhood, from the age of seven, I felt a love for the various branches of learning, and wished to become a religious scholar; until the age of seventeen I was a seeker and searcher for knowledge, but kept to the Twelver [Shi'a] faith of my fathers.'* But under the influence of two Isma'ilis, he proclaimed Isma'ili allegiance in 1072. And after a visit to Cairo, the Isma'ili centre of power, he returned to Persia to spread his beliefs and to reduce the hostile Sunnis.

We continued to climb. To our left, across the deep gorge, the rock sloped upwards in flakes, like a *mille-feuilles* gateau. In front, nothing obscured our view to the opposite side of the valley. We scrambled up the last part, whose surface was dangerously loose, and stood for a moment, trying to get our breath.

The castle is said to have been built by a Dailami king who when hunting one day saw his eagle alight on this rock. Seeing its strategic position, he built the castle, and 'called it Aluh Amut, which in the Daylami language means the eagle's teaching'.† Later, Hasan-i-Sabbah disguised himself, and entering, forced the owner to surrender; but he gave the man a note for three thousand dinars.

Araf conducted me round the top, but there were few remains to look at, for when it gave up to the Mongols, they dismantled its fortifications. At one side, we looked over the edge, but

* B. Lewis, *The Assassins*, London 1967. Quoted from a fragment of Hasan-i-Sabbah's autobiography, preserved by later historians.
† *ibid.*, quoting Ibn al-Athir.

I backed hastily away: it fell for a thousand feet in perpendicular rock.

'Come on, come and look,' said Araf. 'There's water here.'

I crawled to the edge again and saw two gashes about thirty feet below.

'You'll have to go down if you want to look,' he said and began sliding on his bottom. It was quite safe, for a platform caught him, but frightened by the height, I decided not to follow.

'Come on, what's the matter?' he called. 'Are you frightened or what?'

I forced myself to go down and when I reached the shelf I clung to a knob in the rock. Araf jumped to the right and I peered over to the tank. A cistern about twenty feet long and eight feet wide was chiselled out of the rock, like a coffin with its lid half open; the water was green, and it looked deep. The garrison men may have filled these by hand in the summer when rainwater was minimal; but however it was done I did not envy those who had to carry the water up from the tank each day.

The top of the mound was long and narrow, divided into levels by clumps of rock. Near the centre was a cave which was open at both ends, and which looked onto the village below. According to Araf it was the look-out post, so we sat on the floor and gazed out. It was gloomy, out of the sun, and a breeze crept through: I could imagine huddling there in winter, glancing occasionally at the valley to see if an army was approaching. Even in summer, the life must have been hard, for the place seemed barren and relentless. And Hasan-i-Sabbah was austere—during his thirty-four years at Alamut, he left his room only twice, for 'he was occupied with reading books, committing the words of the *da'wa* to writing, and administering the affairs of his realm . . .'*

He sent his wife and daughters away from the fortress for safety, and expected other commanders to do the same; he executed one of his sons for drinking wine, and another on a charge of murder. And he continually sent out followers, to assassinate visitors, princes, and Sunni religious leaders. He had complete authority as the Imam's representative, who according to the Isma'ilis held the secrets to divine understanding: his teaching and commands led all followers to the one eternal truth. And of all commands,

* *ibid.*, quoting Rashid al-Din.

assassination was most glorious, for to kill an infidel, and be killed, meant immediate entry to Paradise.

Beyond the cave was a smooth shoulder, covered with brown stubbled grass. One edge jutted out like a balcony, its sides barred by an earth wall. We walked onto it and looked over, where again there was only sheer cliff.

'Doesn't it worry you?' I asked Araf, who was leaning well forward.

'Not me,' he replied.

'But think of falling over.'

'Who would?' he said scornfully, then added: 'Of course people were made to jump.'

'And this, I suppose, is the garden of Paradise,' I mocked, pointing to the barren slope behind us. He nodded.

One of the commonest myths in Europe was that Hasan-i-Sabbah drugged his followers, placing them in a magnificent garden to give them a foretaste of Paradise, and to make them eager to kill. Marco Polo, without visiting the fortress, described the garden as filled with pavilions and palaces 'and runnels too, flowing freely with wine and milk, and honey and water, and numbers of ladies, and of the most beautiful damsels in the world'.

We took the same path down to regain the village, and Araf's home. His mother was sitting outside stitching a shirt, using her thumb as a thimble. The veins stood out on the back of her hand and along her wrist, and each finger looked like a spatula. She had covered her hair with a white scarf, and sat erect greeting us with a nod.

We went inside and Araf pulled out some cushions from a pile at the back of the room. He saw me looking at the rugs on the floor.

'Home-made,' he said. 'My sisters weave them.'

I ran my hand over the nearest. It was a *gilim*, woven rather than knotted. It was blood-orange in colour interwoven with cobalt-blue diamonds progressing through sea-green oblongs. I was surprised, for the design seemed more typical of tribal rugs, and showed no sign of Islamic influence. But these villagers were not part of a tribe—perhaps it was the effect of the mountains, and of living in such a tightly-knit community so that intricacy was not necessary.

I looked round the room. The walls were thick, indented with shelves for lamps and clothes. There were two windows, both tightly closed with shutters to keep out the heat. The doors were of walnut, almost two inches thick, and elegantly carved like Jacobean panelling: three blocks projected in buttress formation, framed by patterned lines.

His father came in and we bowed to each other. The top of his head was bald, and his deep forehead swept into a conical hat. His hands were covered with hairline scabs, where his skin had cracked and bled. He did not speak but sat while his wife brought in some food. There was rice, and two eggs swimming in oil; he gave one to me and divided the other with Araf. Then Araf brought in a large wooden cot and his mother followed with a baby.

'Is it yours?' I asked.

She burst into laughter. 'What a notion. I haven't had children for years.' She glanced at her husband, and he nodded, continuing to suck his pipe. 'It's my daughter's child,' she said and jogged it up and down till it cried. 'That's it, now, cry away the jinn. Cry, cry. What will you be? Rustam, or Jamshid.'*

She put the child on the cot and bound him to it with some bandages. His arms were also bound so only his head could move, rolling from side to side like a rag doll's. His grandmother sat on the floor, rocking the cradle to and fro. She chuckled at the baby, pushed flies away, and began to hum. I saw the baby fall asleep, then the old man, and when I woke a short while later, she was still sitting, rocking and humming.

I spent some time with the family, for they were friendly and unintrusive. But for two days I had to control my bladder—there were no enclosed lavatories so that the back of the house was used. I did not go in the daytime, for the passers-by were frequent, and at night-time, I was frightened there might be scorpions. Finally, I went for a walk in the hills, but several children followed me. Seeing a hollow beside a boulder, I waved them imperiously on. I at least was grateful for shortage of water in the village, for it meant I had drunk little.

The walks took me into the hills away from the village to explore

---

* Rustam, the great Persian hero; Jamshid, the famous king of Iran in early history. Both are immortalised in Firdausi's epic, *Shah-nameh*.

the ravines and rocks, and when I was on top of a shoulder, I could see for miles: apart from the green valley bottom, which looked like a blade of grass in a man's roughened palm, the mountains seemed uninhabited. They resembled desert mountains, harsh in their contours and remorselessly red. But when I slid down a ridge, I suddenly came to a hamlet with its tiny stream and three or four trees: it seemed secret, and peacefully lazy.

Then climbing another shoulder, I noticed the silence and lack of smell. Here, in the afternoons, nothing moved, neither people nor animals, and no noise drifted up from the hamlets. The ground itself was baked to impotence, its surface encrusted with stones and cracked soil, unrelieved by pungent herbs. I felt insignificant, as though I had no identity, and yet I felt part of this natural order. Perhaps Jesus Christ was right when he said in Qum that the earth, and the mountains which pegged it in place, were the surest signs of God, or at least of some spiritual presence. I felt as though my brain had been washed of irrelevant things, that some veils had been removed. A modern dervish describes beautifully how such veils surround us:

Seventy Thousand Veils separate Allah, the One Reality, from the world of matter and of sense. And every soul passes before his birth through those seventy thousand. The inner half of these are veils of light: the outer half, veils of darkness. For every one of the veils of light passed through, in this journey towards birth, the soul puts *off* a divine quality; and for every one of the dark veils, it puts *on* an earthly quality. Thus the child is born *weeping*, for the soul knows its separation from Allah, the One Reality. And when the child cries in its sleep, it is because the soul remembers something of what it has lost. Otherwise, the passage through the veils has brought with it forgetfulness (nisyān): and for this reason man is called *insān*. He is now, as it were, in prison in his body, separated by these thick curtains from Allah.*

One afternoon Araf and I walked between the village mud walls and haystacks; we crossed a bean field and sat by a stream-bed.
'Is it very difficult to make money here?' I asked.
He shrugged. 'We grow what we need. And my sisters make

* R. A. Nicholson, *The Mystics of Islam*, London 1963.

carpets. Besides we've got the walnut trees.' He spread out his arms to a line of trees.

He picked up a stone and flung it. Two walnuts fell, and I ran over to find them.

'It's all right,' said Araf. 'I'll get them. You knock some more down.'

He peeled away the green outer skins and cracked one nut against another. I tried to do the same, but could not, and he took them from me with a contemptuous grin.

In the evenings, I sat outside the family's home. A path sloped down beside the house and divided into three. It seemed to be the cross-roads of the village: two women gossiped while one of their cows pushed open a gate and chewed the tree inside; three children played tig; a woman walked by with a huge load of twigs, and others had wheat and water. They greeted me cheerfully, some giving me nuts, or whatever they had in their pocket.

On the neighbouring verandah, a woman was suckling her child, unperturbed by my presence. When the child had finished, she buttoned her dress, picked up a bowl and came over. It was filled with orange berries, and taking a handful, she tossed them into her mouth. Then she spat out the pips, and smiling, put the bowl in my lap. I offered some to Araf's mother, who cackled.

'Has that woman been putting a spell on you?'

'I expect she thought I was starving here.'

'Well, I'll have one of her love pills,' and she wrinkled her nose as she sucked the sour fruit.

Araf's married sister helped her mother with supper. She was a large-boned, tall woman who stood with her shoulders back and one leg thrust forward. She had a cotton smock which was gathered at the ribs, and though she was pregnant, she looked childish in it, for the sleeves were far too short. Beneath hung a skirt of knife pleats and her legs were swathed in trousers.

When supper was ready, we moved inside and sat in a circle, including the women. As we picked at the food, I noticed how big the women's hands were, and wide, with long fingers. They worked the rice firmly and rhythmically, carrying a lump to their mouths without dropping a grain. And as I kept dropping my food, they laughed.

One evening, I asked if they would sell some rugs and the girls rushed out to bring a selection. I did not like the colours, so asked if there was one like those on the floor.

'Which one?' said the mother, and I pointed to the orange and sea-green one. She consulted her daughters, then knelt down and rolled up the one I had chosen.

'What are you doing?' I asked.

'Don't you want this one?' she said.

'But it's yours. I can't just take it off your floor.'

'Why not? We've got others.'

'Don't you like it?'

'Yes. But what's a carpet? We'll choose another and like it just as much.'

'Are you sure?'

'Bring the weighing machine,' she called to her husband.

He brought in a pair of balancing scales—two rusty tin cans attached either end of a stick. He balanced the carpet on one tin, and dropped large stones in the other. He and Araf lifted the stick, to see if the cans balanced, but the carpet hung lower, so he added more stones. When the cans were roughly even, he set them down, and weighed the stones in his hand.

'Half a kilo, that one. A quarter. A kilo. This one must be one and a half. What do you think?' He gave me the stone.

'About eight grammes over,' I said, having no idea of its weight.

The old man finished counting. 'That makes nine kilos near enough.'

We bargained about the number of kilos, and then we bargained about the price per kilo. When we had finished, we sat drinking tea as though nothing had happened. The bare patch remained on the floor.

One morning I set off by myself to climb a hill I had picked out in the distance. It was early, and the gullies of the hills were black still, unexposed by sun, but above, the peaks sucked in the red sky and then slowly baked to russet. I kept to the ridges where occasionally I found a path; but as it grew hotter, I dropped down into the shaded ravines.

After a few hours' walking, I came to a hamlet and a woman gave me some water. One of her front teeth was missing, but the rest were white and strong. A child ran out from the house, and seeing me, hid behind her mother's skirts.

'Have you other children?' I asked.

She nodded. 'Four. But the boys have gone to the towns.'

It suddenly occurred to me that I had seen few young men in the other villages and hamlets—girls, yes, and old men working in the fields.

'But they come back to help with the harvest?'

'Sometimes. But they have their work. They bring us money you know.'

She seemed unperturbed that the money was destroying her family, but perhaps she merely accepted it with fortitude as God's irrevocable will.

I continued up the slopes. The walking was fairly easy, for the ground was even, though dusty; yet sometimes I had to climb over huge boulders or make a detour round a cliff to the next layer of hills. Not far from here, I thought, the hero Zal was abandoned when still a baby, for he had been born with white hair which had shamed his father. He was left on the mountain without food or water, but a Simurg, the legendary Persian bird, swooped on him and carried him back to its nest. There he was raised on blood, until his father, warned in a dream of his son's survival, rescued him. But Zal's main claim to fame in the legends of Iran, is that he fathered the mighty Rustam.

I did not reach my hill, for it grew too hot, and I eventually returned to the village of Alamut as it was growing dark. The family had already eaten, but had saved a large plateful for me. We prepared for bed, and the old man began to say his prayers. It seemed that none of the family said prayers regularly—perhaps here in the mountains they did not feel the need to approach their God with words.

The next morning at five o'clock, I said goodbye to the family, for I had decided it was time to leave Alamut. But first I wanted to see Maymundiz, another stronghold further west, which helped control the key route from Qazvin to the Caspian. Fortunately, Araf said he would act as my guide.

We had about six miles to walk, so he took the mule for my bag and the carpet. We trudged up through the village, and turned into an inverted tunnel. The top of the pass was lit by the sun and the shadows were slowly receding towards us. It was a steady ascent, and the ground was even, till the land sank in a ravine, then soared on the other side. We scrambled to the bottom, and plodded upwards for more than an hour till suddenly we were on the top. A corrie, a huge bowl, tilted into the mountain like the mouth of a crater, its sides sloping evenly down. I could see for miles, the hills crinkled like the skin of boiled milk; and still they were empty—not a tree, not a shrub, not the shimmer of heat.

At the bottom we came to a village, tucked into a cliff by the side of a river. The stone walls were often dislodged by the brambles which trailed over them. The place seemed deserted, almost eerie, and we saw no-one till the other side of the village.

We followed the river through rock obelisks which were corroded as though by torrents. We washed our faces in the icy water and ate the cheese I had brought. There was a gap between the rocks nearby but it ended in a cul-de-sac. We entered nonetheless and struggled up the face on a path of sliding stones. At the top was a grass-covered bowl with trees, and from its brim, the land rolled away like a steppe. We saw a flock of sheep and a young boy whistling. A man jogged by, his mule laden with sacks. Then some women passed, goading their white donkeys with switches and high-pitched curses.

Araf pointed to the mound of Maymundiz. It was like a tinned loaf which had been pecked by birds, somewhat stale and pink. Near the bulk of rock was the village of Shams Kilaya, straddling a dry river bed. Beyond it, we tied the mule to a shrine wall and scrambled up a slope. It was not very high, but steep and covered with scree and plants with flimsy roots. We sat at the base of the rock: about twenty feet above us were the fortress openings which led to rooms and stables hewn out of solid rock. We had no means of getting up there, and I remembered the expedition, whose slides I had seen at school, had spent days making ladders.

The fortress had been built by Hasan-i-Sabbah's successor; but a hundred years later, from Maymundiz, the Isma'ili leader surrendered to Hulagu Khan. It seemed the end of the Persian Isma'ilis, for he and his family were murdered. But in the nineteenth century, the leaders re-emerged, the succession secured by a son whom they claimed had survived.

In 1818, the Shah of Persia appointed one leader as governor of Qum, and gave him the title of Aga Khan. But he rebelled, unsuccessfully, and fled to India. In 1866, as the result of a trial involving Isma'ilis, whose origins had to be researched, the Chief Justice of Bombay, Sir Joseph Arnould, pronounced the Aga Khan as 'spiritual head of the Isma'ilis and heir of the Imams of Alamut.'*

'What time does the bus go back to Qazvin?' I asked.

'Half-past two,' said Araf.

I looked at my watch—it was two o'clock. We slid down to the shrine and stumbled along the river bed; ran through the village, and crossed a field which was sliced with trenches, to arrive on the road. An old man was quietly loading a donkey and a lorry stood empty nearby. There was no such thing as a bus.

I walked over to a brick hut where a slouching man was swilling a teapot into the gutter.

'Has the bus gone?' I asked, hastily, without greeting.

The man stood up slowly and stared. 'What bus?'

'The one for Qazvin. Has it gone?'

'There's no bus today.'

'But my friend said there was.'

'I expect there'll be one tomorrow,' he answered.

We sat at one of the tables outside and the owner brought tea and a bowl of grapes. I pointed to the lorry.

'Is that going to Qazvin?'

He wiped two saucers with a dirty cloth. 'That's been there for three days. It's broken down. But there's a lorry passing in half an hour.'

'Oh that's fine then.'

A man at another table stared at us. He was wearing a pin-stripe suit which was frayed and blotched with dirt. His eyes were blood-shot and sunken.

'Going to Qazvin are you?' he asked.

'That's the plan,' I answered.

'There's no bus today,' he said.

'No, I know.'

'There may be a lorry.'

'Thank you, yes, I thought there was.'

'It'll be along in half an hour.'

We finished our tea and Araf stood up to leave.

* B. Lewis: *The Assassins*, London 1967.

I gave him some money, and placing my things on a chair, he mounted the mule and rode off.

An hour went by; I stood up to see if there was dust in the distance. There was nothing.

'Are you sure there's a lorry today?' I asked the proprietor.

'What's bothering you? It'll come. If it doesn't come today, it'll come tomorrow.' And he gave me more tea.

To my surprise a lorry arrived and pulled up in front of the tea-house. The driver jumped down and strutted towards us: he was wearing a bright plaid shirt, his shoulders bent forward. His hands touched the front of his thighs, half-clenched as though waiting to punch an opponent.

His assistant ambled behind, a lanky man with a large white shirt which made him look padded. His face was long, with a soft mouth, and his hair was swept back from his forehead, backcombed for extra height.

The driver slapped the proprietor's back. 'How's business, you old rich man? Got important guests? Pays well, does he?'

'Tea?' said the owner, putting two glasses on the table. 'That young man wants a lift to Qazvin.'

'Of course, we'll take him for a sum.'

Twenty minutes later we set off. The lorry was like a cattle truck that had seen forty years of service. The wheels were bald, the body work dented, and its brake pedal repaired with tape. We collected eight passengers from a village; they sat on the roof of the cabin, their legs dangling over the windscreen.

I was put in front with an old man, and the driver began a love song, shouting the words above the engine. When he reached a high note, he turned to look at us, beating his hand on his chest. The old man tapped his head and pointed to the driver: I nodded with a grin and then turned to the driver and winked.

We were going down a steep slope, the driver pumping the brakes ineffectually. He crashed into a lower gear, not using the clutch, which was broken. The lorry swerved to the edge of the road. He pulled on the handbrake heavily and we stopped at the bottom with a puncture.

I wandered away while the wheel was being repaired. The sun was approaching the peaks so that the hills were marbled with shadow. A few stars showed directly above me where the sky had deepened to indigo, and one glistened to the west near the sun.

When we got into the lorry again, I climbed onto the top.

'Had enough of him?' asked the old man, pertinently.

'I just like looking at stars.'

'Tell me my fortune then,' yelled the driver and we began the long ascent. His assistant was sitting beside me, shivering, so I pulled a jersey from my bag.

'Here, wear this.'

'Don't you want it?' he asked.

'No, I'm fine.'

He pulled it over his head and arranged the end of the sleeves; he took out a comb and put his hair into place. Then he lifted the front of the jersey to his nose.

'Mm, smells nice,' he said.

I laughed. 'It's never been worn.'

'Oh, I thought it was your smell.'

We lay back and watched the stars, tracing them out with our fingers.

'You don't have girlfriends?' asked Hasan, suddenly taking hold of my hand. 'What soft hands you've got.' I knew they were rough, and quickly tucked them into my pockets. But I had no particular feeling towards him—I suppose my constant suppression of feelings towards men and women had made me into a true eunuch.

By the time we reached the top of the pass, it was dark, and we could see the large circle of Qazvin's lights. Hasan clapped his hands and began singing, trilling delicately on every note. When he had finished a phrase, the driver bawled it back from the cabin. Suddenly the driver yelled, and swerving, jerked the lorry to a halt. A cardboard box lay in the middle of the road, and the passengers ran back to open it. It was empty, so they kicked it aside. Two hundred yards on was another box: 'Get it, get it,' yelled everyone, and the lorry scored, nearly turning itself over.

We reached the terminus in Qazvin, and jumping down, I pulled out some money.

'That's all right,' said the driver. 'No money.'

'But please, I want to pay something.'

Hasan was taking off my jersey. 'Come and have supper with me instead.'

'But I've got to get back to Tehran,' I lied.

'Well you'd better be off,' said the driver, nearly crushing my hand as he shook it.

I put out my hand to Hasan. He took hold of my face and kissed me hard on the mouth.

I found a hotel whose washroom door I could lock, and stripped down to clean myself thoroughly. I was itching all over, from fleas and mosquitoes, and my body looked diseased by pox. I started to count the number of bites, but gave up when I reached two hundred. I felt like Thackeray's limerick:

> There's a wealthy old man of Tabreez
> With a maudlin affection for fleas,
>   He'll grin with delight
>   When they scratch him and bite—
> Perverted old man of Tabreez.

I was beginning to feel overwhelmed by all that I had experienced, and rather than see anything more, I wanted to stand back, to try and put my impressions into perspective. But my main feeling was one of confusion, so that I found it hard to draw conclusions, or even to draw together the multiple strands I had gathered. Besides, the country seemed composed of far more strands than I had seen, so that my thoughts on its character only skimmed reality.

Patterns and colours—those were the two things which kept recurring in my mind. Not just the patterns, the tracery, flowing over surfaces—the arabesques and flowers, the scrollwork and lettering; nor just the vivid turquoise and yellow juxtaposed with the brown of the earth. But patterns of life, of faith, of speech, which seemed to intermingle but not to unite: a tribeswoman in scarlet skirts, made independent by the demands of mountains; a townswoman concealed in her black veil, and enclosed from society by high mud walls; the rarefied atmosphere of Qum, where closeness to God seemed the main ambition; the dependence on God of villagers, whose survival was sometimes near to destruction. Perhaps these images were too simplistic, too strongly contradictory, so that I could see little unity between them. They seemed only a mass of loose threads, crossing and recrossing without order, imposed on one country by political boundaries.

Yet as I thought further, I felt increasingly that there was unity which merely expressed itself in different ways. It seemed like a Persian carpet—an obvious symbol, but I hope still valid—where lines wind separately, yet form a patterned whole. And with Iran, I felt such unity might stem from Islam, whose influence penetrated the daily lives of the people, so their speech, their actions, their art, reflected a feeling for God. Perhaps I was thinking more of the rural areas, where materialism had not yet ousted faith, but even in the towns, it had seemed that Islam was not forgotten.

But then I felt there was a force even greater than Islam which brought unity—something almost intangible, the essence rather than the factor. For despite innumerable invasions, from the Greeks, the Arabs, the Mongols, and now the West, Iran seemed to have retained her own identity, adapting maybe, but interpreting everything in her way, so that her character remained firm: sometimes sensual and cruel, but generally sophisticated, with a strong regard for detail and delicacy, intrigue and intricacy. Perhaps it was her very diversity which provided her unity, though not uniformity; for 'Unity requires a difference in all things. Uniformity requires congruency. Unity is strong, beautiful, flexible; Uniformity is rigid and colourless.'*

I decided to leave for home, for in addition I was longing to put into practice the designs I had studied, and to experiment with colour and texture. But before leaving, I returned to Qum to see Jesus Christ and Hasan-'Ali. I went to the *madraseh* opposite the shrine, but as Hasan-'Ali was not there, I walked to his *madraseh* in the old part of the town. His room was locked, but the other students greeted me and gave me another room. They brought food, and as it grew dark, came to talk.

'Don't you pray?' asked a young boy, as the calls to God filled the courtyard.

'What do you think of Bertrand Russell?' asked another man who was holding a thick volume of Russell's work. He read a passage. 'I find he's clever, sometimes wise, but he often misses the truth.'

'What sort of carpets do your churches have?'

* David Hofman, *The Renewal of Civilization*, London 1946.

'Tell me about the Presbyterians. Why did they break away?'

'How many years does a Christian mulla study? Does he know the Bible by heart?'

Then Hasan-'Ali arrived, having heard in the centre of town that I had come. Was I all right? Why had I been to the college? Didn't I know that some of the students disliked Europeans? I was surprised: it was the only time I was ever aware of such feeling in Qum.

Immediately we went to Jesus Christ's house, and when we had settled on the floor, they asked what I had done, what I had seen. They smiled when I recounted with fervour my feelings for the mountains; they nodded when I talked of the Turkmen wedding; they laughed at Mephistopheles' tantrums.

'But what have you been doing?' I asked.

'Nothing so exciting,' said Jesus Christ, smiling. 'I don't think you need to ask. We pray, we reflect, we discuss. We try to act rightly in God's way, and to understand the truth. Just as you, in your way, have been trying to understand.'

'But I understand little. I'm only confused. Perhaps my very movement prevented it.'

'I don't think so. We all work differently, but whatever our path, we work towards the same understanding, the same truth. But it takes time, it takes love and devotion, and much effort. Can we expect to gain if we do not work? And can we expect to gain if we are full of wrong thoughts and impurities?'

His words, though more direct, reminded me of part of a poem.

> Like sheaves of corn [Love] gathers you unto himself.
> He threshes you to make you naked.
> He sifts you to free you from your husks.
> He grinds you to whiteness.
> He kneads you until you are pliant;
> And then he assigns you to his sacred fire, that you may
>   become sacred bread for God's sacred feast.*

'Love,' said Jesus Christ. 'And patience. How can we learn and understand if we block out such things? And we can understand, we can learn, for God gave us the ability to think and reason. If only we could reflect His great beauty! There is a mystic tale of Rumi's, which is relevant, I think:

* Kahlil Gibran, *The Prophet*, London 1964.

'Once some Chinese and Greek artists were arguing, each group claiming that they were the better artists. So the Sultan shut them in separate rooms to prove themselves. The Chinese asked for hundreds of colours, and painted for days an elaborate and sensitive picture. The Greeks on the other hand merely polished the walls, until they became smooth and clear. For indeed, colour is like the clouds, but lack of colour is like the moon. If you see magnificent colours filtering through the clouds, then know that they come from the sun, the moon or the stars.

'Soon the Chinese had finished, and called for the king. When he entered their room, he was overcome by the beauty of their work. Then he went into the room of the Greeks, who drew back the curtain between the rooms, so that the picture of the Chinese was reflected in even greater glory.

'This purity of the mirror is surely the heart, cleansed of all impurities, so that whatever images it receives, it can throw them back again in perfection.'

The next day, the three of us left in a taxi for Tehran, accompanied by two mullas, for Jesus Christ was going to an Islamic Conference in Delhi. It still felt a strange experience, driving through arid countryside wedged between men whose robes filled most of the seat, and where the view of passing scenery was restricted by turbans and beards. The noise of the taxi prevented much talking, and at one moment, Jesus Christ took hold of my arm to attract my attention. His fingers just touched my flattened breast. I must have shrunk away, for he withdrew his hand and apologised.

'English men don't like being touched by other men,' he commented.

I nodded and thought how the men in Qum embraced each other and held hands with no undertones of homosexuality; and I remembered how often I had had firmly to stretch out my hand for a handshake, to prevent an embrace.

When we reached Tehran, we agreed that I would join them that evening at their hotel to say a final goodbye. It was an unfriendly place, sparsely furnished, with green walls and stone floors, and seemed to cater specifically for religious men and pilgrims. I arrived after dark and the man behind the desk eyed me with suspicion when I asked for Jesus Christ and Hasan-'Ali.

Four iron bedsteads lined their room. Jesus Christ and one of
the mullas were seated on one, so I took off my shoes and sat
facing them.

'Let's order something to eat,' said Hasan-'Ali, and the mulla
went out to buy it.

'Mind you bring the right thing back,' called Jesus Christ. He
turned to me. 'There was once a man who was told to buy some
cream, but he misunderstood, and came back with a prostitute.'

'Did the good man send her away?' asked Hasan-'Ali.

'No, he kept her to look after his children, to make them as
beautiful as possible.'

'They must have got a rich dowry then.'

'Not very. One was blind and the other limped. That was why
he'd kept the woman, to improve what they had.'

I laughed. 'You're getting very flippant. Tehran must be affecting you.'

'No, John, it's not like that. But I sense that now you're leaving,
you have other things to think of, and do not wish to talk about
God. Besides, we mustn't always press our beliefs on you.'

'No, there are still lots of things I want to ask you. And throughout, you've only been telling me what you believe, and not what I
must believe.'

'That's true, but you must choose your own path. And though
I believe Islam is the right path, we mustn't influence you, nor
would we wish to. There's just one thing though.'

'What's that?'

He clasped his hands and looked straight at me. 'Don't tell your
friends in England you cheated us.'

I was startled. 'What do you mean?'

'I think you know what I mean.'

He did not smile and I could not answer.

Hasan-'Ali stood up and left the room; Jesus Christ followed
and left me alone. A few minutes later they returned with two small
packages.

'We've got some good memories of Qum for you,' said Hasan-
'Ali.

I opened the first packet to find a pair of brown socks.

'So you noticed I only had one pair,' I said with delight. 'Or did
you smell them?' And I changed them immediately.

Then I opened Jesus Christ's packet. To my dismay, it was a scarlet nylon petticoat with a white lace hem and plunging neckline. I tried to look lascivious.

'Thank you. It'll suit my future bride very well,' I said with embarrassment.

'Will you ask us to your wedding then?' he asked.

'Yes, of course.' Perhaps that was when I would tell them the truth.

I gave them a present of Indian tea, but they persisted with their questions.

'And she'll be a rose?' asked Hasan-'Ali. 'Then you can fill your nose with sweetest perfumes?'

'Will you wear those clothes?' asked Jesus Christ, curiously. 'You know, I could have lent you a change of shirt in Qum.'

'No, no. I'll have gay clothes, and a big silk tie.'

'And we can come in our robes?' said Hasan-'Ali.

'Of course. Why not?'

'Poor boy,' said Jesus Christ. 'We mustn't tease him. But I'd like to ask one more question.'

'Yes?'

'And you will answer truthfully?'

I hesitated, for I suddenly knew what he would ask. Should I continue to lie? But I knew I respected our friendship too much.

'Yes, I'll be truthful.'

'Then are you a boy or a girl?'

I said, slowly: 'I'm a girl, Jesus Christ, and I wish you hadn't asked. I'm sorry, really sorry. I've offended all your principles. And I've knowingly gone against all your beliefs, and that's unforgivable.'

Jesus Christ nodded. 'I'd thought it so, and I'm glad you were honest. I'm only sorry we haven't treated you with the respect we like to show women.'

'But why didn't you ask before?'

'Why should we have done? We thought you must be a boy. Besides, it was my duty to answer your questions, to help you, and not to put obstacles in your way. But then, when you left, we had time to reflect, and several things made us doubt.'

'What were your doubts?'

'First your laughter, for men seldom laugh silently, moving

their shoulders up and down; but rather they laugh boisterously. Also you use your hands in too feminine a way.'

'And what were my other mistakes?'

'It's good to cast down your eyes, or to open them wide in surprise, but men rarely do it.'

'Did I do that?' I asked.

They both laughed. 'They're wide open now.'

'I've a truthful idea,' said Hasan-'Ali. 'Let's call her Maryam. Mary conceived a boy without a husband and so did this one.'

'And Mary was the one who sat and listened to Jesus while Martha did the work,' added Jesus Christ. 'I'm sorry I left you by yourself, Maryam, a short while ago. I felt you were a girl, and it's not good to sit alone with a woman who isn't your wife.'

'Does it matter that I'm sitting with you now?' I asked.

'No, no please stay. Pursuit of the truth is more important, as I said before, and it's not for me to turn anyone away.'

Perhaps this was the resolution for which I had really been hoping: the establishment of truth between us seemed far more important than the success of a masquerade. My disguise had been meant as an aid, and not as a means or a proof in itself; and now there was no longer need for it, I was glad to discard it— though with some ambivalence, I realised it would take time to return to my normal self. But I was much more glad for the tolerance Jesus Christ had shown of my disguise, and later, when I returned to England, such tolerance was confirmed. For I wrote to them about this book, asking permission to include a chapter on Qum; but I said I would respect their wishes if they did not wish me to describe my 'cheating'. They answered promptly:

About Islam and your experience in Qum, we don't mind at all, but don't you think that before you declare your views and opinions about Islam, you should broaden your knowledge and have a deep study and outlook about Islam. Only a slide and bird's eye view you had here in Qum. By the way you are independent to express your views about Islam, but be careful to look properly before you leap.

Such tolerance and guidance helped, I think, to define my attitude towards Islam, at least in Iran. For in Jesus Christ and

Hasan-'Ali I could see the direct effect of their faith, its sincerity and warmth, its practicality and humour. A religion may suit a man, but I felt Islam was a religion to suit human beings, both physically and spiritually, so that even if a man is not a Muslim, or does not believe in God, he may still benefit if he looks at its teachings.

In another letter, Hasan-'Ali expressed gently something of my feelings:

Please do ponder much in yourself: 'The inner universe' and 'The Book of life'. Observe deeply 'Humanity', its problems and puzzles and try to search out the ways of solving them. Try to think properly—the source of right action is right thinking. Enlighten yourself and then your environment. A muslim is a real man—and a real man who loves and acts on facts is Muslim.

9 *NEW PERCEPTIONS*

For several years, my memories of Qum, Sakina, and the mountains, dominated my ideas about Iran; and when I returned to revisit them some four years after my first journey, my feelings were strengthened into greater respect and affection.

I was puzzled by one or two things, though. Sakina seemed poorer, not richer, despite the claims of impressive national improvements. The village facilities were still undeveloped: there was no road apart from the donkey track, no electricity, no water beyond the tiny spring which had fed the village for decades. And now the village was under threat from a scheme to extend the lake—not in order to provide irrigation, but to form part of a royal game park.

In Qum, I discovered that Jesus Christ had gone to teach in Qatar. But his absence, and my new veiled role as a woman, did not deter others from showing me hospitality. I was taken to see Ayatullah Shariat-Madari, the leading divine in Iran. He was a frail and gentle patriarch with a delicate sense of humour. Perhaps I was prejudiced in my reaction, but many have said the same. And although his pronouncements were guarded, and even conservative, he possessed both knowledge and wisdom, and could never be termed reactionary. Yet the Shah repeatedly claimed that there was not an Islamic representative with whom he could talk about plans for Iran's development and the role of religion within society.

Gradually, both myself and my interests were changing. I had found contentment at home and I no longer felt the need to try to find an identity. I still wanted to learn and to understand, particularly about human beings as Hasan-'Ali suggested, but I did not wish for adventure in itself. I also learnt to explore the conditions of those with restricted material resources by living for months with a peasant family in southern India.

The challenge seemed greater for any such intimate study within Iran. There was a prevaricating bureaucracy which had to approve all research permits: there was surveillance by SAVAK, the secret intelligence agency, and control in the rural areas by the Imperial Iranian Gendarmerie; there was fear on the part of ordinary people to reveal their feelings, especially to an unknown foreigner; and there was always the problem of moving about now that I was a woman. Perhaps a loss of innocence made it harder to delude.

Yet the more I returned to Iran, and the more I learnt from others, the more I wanted to carry out a detailed human study. The attempts at technical modernisation, the veneer of westernisation, an over-burdening regime—all were presented as necessary and in the end beneficial. Few spoke of the stress involved, and few analysed the process of change that affected the whole society.

I realised the extent of internal tension when I went to Iran early in 1978. Demonstrations leading to clashes occurred in Qum after the denunciation of the religious leader, Ayatullah Khumaini, in a national newspaper. The Shah stated that six people were killed; Ayatullah Shariat-Madari swore on the Quran that he had personally seen fifteen corpses brought into his hospital in Qum; other eye-witnesses claimed that more than fifty people were dead but that bodies had been bundled away in police-vans to prevent a final count.

By September, when I returned again, thousands of people were out on the streets to mourn more dead and to denounce the Shah. I sensed it was also an explosion against excessive corruption, inflation, the misdirection of oil funds, thoughtless modernity, inappropriate secularity, intellectual and political oppression, the disruption of family, plus the loss of traditions which were valued by more than conservative elements. It was expressed in religious fervour, in which deep frustration translated itself into martyrdom. But for some, Islam was only the means of protest and was not the ultimate goal.

On September 8th, martial law was declared in twelve cities throughout the country, including Tehran. Unaware of the new regulations, thousands of unarmed people had gathered in east Tehran. The army was brought in against them, in force. Official figures stated eighty-six dead; the Western press cautiously numbered several hundred; others observed that over a thousand were killed both by machine-gun and from helicopters.

That evening, secure in the north of Tehran, I noticed the silence of curfew. It was unnatural and somehow sinister. No traffic, no people, no bustle, only a tank or military jeep occasionally trundling by. Even a village has noise at night, but my street was utterly silent.

I could not sleep through the night. I kept thinking that only a few miles away people were dying from wounds, bodies were being secretly buried, buildings were burning, women and men were weeping. Iranian had killed Iranian, with the help of Western weaponry.

And also I knew that all this had happened before in Iran, not as part of past history, but within the last eighty years, over and over again, as part of living memory.

In 1906, there was extensive uprising in the main cities of Iran. It was led by the mullas and merchants demanding law and justice. A parliament and constitution were quickly assembled, but within two years, the parliament was bombarded and some of the most outstanding leaders killed by royalist troops backed by Imperial Russia.

There was spasmodic civil war in the north of Iran for several years after that. In the south, the British discovered oil and quietly began to extract it. But on the outbreak of World War I, despite Iran's declared neutrality, British troops occupied the country in order to protect the oil-fields. They stayed for seven years. The Russians also strengthened their position until they had to withdraw because of their revolution.

The 20s saw the rise of Reza Khan and his coronation as first Shah of the Pahlavi dynasty. Hopes were high for the end of disorder. Though his rule brought stability and prosperity for some, his increasingly authoritarian approach created an oppressive burden for large sections of society. Many died in the process.

In 1941, there was yet another invasion from British and Russian troops. The Americans also moved in troops, and none withdrew until 1946.

There was a new Shah; there were twenty-three cabinets in ten years; upheavals in the provinces; separatist movements; a ruined economy, due to the occupation; there were famine and epidemics. In 1951, on a wave of popular support, Dr. Mosaddeq nationalised oil and effectively ruled the country as prime minister; in 1953, with riots against him, the Shah was forced to leave the country; but within days he returned with the help of the CIA and with the support of further riots. He cleaned the country of 'communists' and set up his secret intelligence service advised by the FBI and the CIA, along with British intelligence.

Early in the 60s, again there was unrest, and more riots, both in cities and countryside, against the introduction of land reform. The army clashed with civilians. Hundreds were killed; hundreds more were imprisoned. Nobody knows the total.

And through all the political turbulence, there were still the problems of poverty, hunger, disease, illiteracy, and limited material resources. It is hardly surprising that a sense of insecurity pervades Iranian society. And it has not been helped by the sudden influx of oil revenues in the 70s that led to a scramble for wealth, a massive build-up of weaponry, and an increasing gap between rich and poor.

Two days after the tragic shootings, a friend drove me to Qum. We passed through the south of Tehran: the shops were open, and trade seemed normal, but at the entrance to the bazaar stood a heavily manned tank, with soldiers at the ready. Women passed by on their way to shop, their heads bent, their bodies and faces shrouded in thick black veils.

Once on the open road we relaxed, no longer controlled by martial law. We overtook an army vehicle that had carried a tank to Tehran and now was returning to base; we came to another, and another, and passed nine in half an hour.

On approaching Qum, I put on my veil. Almost all the shops were shuttered, and the streets were nearly empty. Two armoured cars stood in the main square, their soldiers at the ready. The city was under martial law.

I was dropped at a new hotel with smoked glass doors and a modern lobby with huge plastic chairs for lounging. My room had a comfortable bed, a wash-basin and a telephone. It was hardly the Qum I knew.

I stayed in my room except when visiting friends. They proposed that I meet Ayatullah Shariat-Madari, but it was hardly the appropriate time. He was receiving those who had travelled from Tehran to give eye-witness reports of the killings. He was said to be deeply distressed, but still he insisted that no-one should turn to violence. Indeed he issued a communique stating simply that there were forces at work to destroy Islamic unity; that people should keep to the Islamic law; and that no-one should trust all they heard or read in the news.

It was hardly incitement to revolution; yet Ayatullah Shariat-Madari only six months before had been rushed into hospital with a heart-attack after two mullas who ran into his house for sanctuary were shot dead by police in his presence. The turban from one of those killed lay on the carpet for weeks as witness to the violation of the unwritten laws of protection.

It is easy to forget when confronted by the passion Ayatullah Khumaini has invoked and the power he has subsequently gained that there are other spokesmen for Islam within Iran.

The variety of Islamic studies means a variety of religious representatives in a variety of fields, from theology and jurisprudence to history, philosophy, science, medicine, languages, and literature. Their knowledge, their attitudes, and their loyalties differ and sometimes conflict. They have different responsibilities within society, both at the practical and spiritual levels.

There is no official hierarchy among leaders in Shi'a Islam, as in the Catholic or Protestant church—there is no ordination and no power structure culminating in the equivalent of one Pope or one Archbishop. Instead, the scholars, the religious leaders, and the mullas emerge according to ability, popularity, and a process of consensus among others. Consequently, a number of Ayatullahs can also emerge at one time. They have different personalities, different areas of interest, and they expound their knowledge to whomever chooses to listen. In the revolution of 1906, for example, many mullas led the demands for reform and justice; but religious leaders also supported the king in the fight against constitutionalism.

In Iran, it is the individual from king to peasant who can select—or not, as the case may be—those religious leaders whom he respects, who share his concerns, and whose advice helps him to resolve his problems. He also selects one Ayatullah as his religious authority. For many, of course, the choice is pre-determined by the pressures of society and long-standing tradition; but for others—both men and women—the choice is very real, particularly for those uprooted from their homes, like the migrants to cities, the new middle class, the students, and the new economic elite.

The hotel was comfortable and air-conditioned, yet I could not sleep soundly. Once I woke abruptly to hear shouts outside my window. A soldier was marching a man across the street. I heard more voices below. A door opened and shut. Then a jeep drew up and soldiers got out. I could not see, but I thought they entered the hotel. I heard voices in the foyer, and people on the stairs. I was extremely frightened. I got out of bed and wrapped my long veil around me. I waited. The voices stopped, the steps receded. I climbed back into bed.

The shops stayed closed in Qum, and when I returned to Tehran, the bazaar also had closed despite military threats.

I found it extraordinary how quickly and comprehensively the bazaars shut down, not just in one town, but across the whole country. It cost the merchants much money, but it caused immense disruption, for the bazaars were the main distributors of food supplies to the cities. But the bazaar in Iran has never been simply a market: it is a political and social network whose activities are defined in religious terms, whether for financial transactions, social behaviour, or supporting the clergy in religious activities. It is also one of the few networks that has consistently defied the governing classes, for it has solidarity and wealth, and is good for communication.

I wanted to walk through the endless alleys to see the effect of closure, but I did not have the courage: the xenophobia that once had been common in the bazaar seemed to have been reawakened, expressing itself in fervour.

In the 60s and 70s, many of the middle-class merchants moved out of the bazaar into a new prosperity; and when imports dominated trade in other parts of the cities, it seemed the bazaar was losing its role as a nerve-centre. But thousands of men and women were migrating from the villages: they were absorbed into the poorer parts of the cities and into the network of mosque, bazaar, and mullas. Allegiance to God, not king, was encouraged by the deterioration in living conditions, limited opportunities, rampant inflation, a clamp-down on political participation, and the neglect of traditional cultural expression. Women put *on* the veil; rituals and sermons grew in importance and impact; passions were soon aroused, given the traditions of Shi'a Islam and its constant recall of martyrdom.

It was different in the countryside, for there were no demonstrations or riots. But there was disillusion at the failure of government to help the rural areas. Thousands and thousands of men had left for the city, sometimes taking their families, sometimes leaving them in the villages to work the land on their behalf. And as in the town, so in the village, religion provided a panacea for those who chose to follow. Cassette recordings of sermons and rituals passed from village to village, and relatives in the city brought back further news. For many, though, remote in mountain or desert, the problems of the towns seemed far removed from the needs of the rural areas.

I was thrilled to get out of Tehran and to drive for miles along empty roads accompanied by a girl-friend who peeled our supply of peaches and pomegranates. I was still haunted by the landscape—the layers and layers of mountain, barren, huge, magnificent; the rarefied light; the brilliant sun; the distant cluster of villages; rich pockets of vegetation. We crossed ridges of hills that were empty and waterless, then dropped down into the plains to find fields and habitation; we wound up through other mountains whose valleys were green from water; we drove through miles of desert. And wherever we went there were pockets of population which had their own identity and their own pattern of living.

Whenever we passed other cars or lorries, the male drivers hooted and waved. A woman driving a car was rare; but two women alone in a car in their veils was almost a sight unseen.

I found the veil an enormous benefit, though as a garment it seemed inefficient for it required the mouth or a hand to prevent it slipping away from the head. It encompassed my whole body, and I found it gave me my own territory which strangers could not intrude on. It also prevented propositioning, because the way I learnt to wear it, plus the colour and weight of the veil, signalled me as a modest woman uninterested in flirtation. I also hadn't to worry about the Western clothes I wore, however stained and dirty, for none of them ever showed. And the veil, in a funny way, made me feel more secure in a climate that was volatile, not just because of the dominant male but because of political instability, social uncertainties, and geographical rawness—affecting women and men alike.

The use of the veil was my personal choice, but for many Iranian women its use is enforced by custom. Such custom is not always Muslim. Once, full veiling was used to some extent as a status symbol by the upper and middle urban classes; but in the 60s and 70s, the *lack* of the veil symbolised wealth and modernity. The strange thing is that the lack of a veil, whether for rich or poor, is not always a sign of emancipation. The unwritten laws of seclusion can still be just as strong.

Although I was now a woman, and could talk more freely with women, I still found it hard to judge the effect of Islam on women. It is true that I felt oppressed at times, but I am sure it had more to do with political instability than with Islamic influence. I do know that certain legal and social rights of women are curtailed by the laws of Islam; but the more I travelled around, the more I felt that the condition of many women within Iran was not very different from that of others around the world—regardless of religion. It seemed to me that, for those with limited material resources, the emphasis for women was frequently on virginity, marriage, fecundity, and the bearing of boys; on domestic activity; on separation from almost all men. Extensive formal education was not considered functional, either by men or women; work outside the home was restricted to certain areas. For those with more wealth, the emphasis was frequently still on marriage, fecundity and domestic activity; but there was a wider choice of education, jobs, and decisions, with greater means for self-beautification.

I know it is dangerous to generalise, but I felt that things weren't as bad as they seemed: the role of the woman within the Iranian family was often more flexible and less subordinate than in some non-Muslim families with whom I have lived elsewhere.

When I arrived at Sakina's home, she squeezed my cheeks to see how thin I had grown, and then she put on the water to boil for tea. Within moments, she was in tears. Her daughter had married a cousin—a good man who treated her well—but only six months after the wedding, while trying to mend a sewage leak, he had slipped in the pit and drowned. At the time her daughter was pregnant and two months later delivered a son.

Sakina was nervous with worry. She couldn't afford another wedding, yet her daughter had to remarry. A woman alone was not acceptable—she offered a threat to established wives, for she could according to Islamic law become an additional wife, and according to Shi'a law she could also become a temporary wife. Besides, a woman alone was more vulnerable to male assault, and already the village was talking and calling her daughter names, so who would want to marry her? The dead husband's brother said he would take her on as a second wife and adopt the son as his own; but Sakina did not like him, nor did her daughter.

Sakina cried often during my stay as she talked of her life in detail. She admitted that the blind old man who shared her house was not her father at all, but her third husband. Her own parents had died when she was young, so her brothers had married her off as soon as possible to a man in the neigbouring village. She bore him four children, but two died, and then her husband died. Her brothers found her another husband but he was an old man with a wife already, so Sakina took second place in the household. She bore him two children, but then he died also, and his relatives made sure that no property or money passed into the hands of Sakina.

Her brothers would do nothing to help, and with two young children to look after, Sakina was nearly destitute. When she received a proposal of marriage from a man who was meant to be wealthy, but who was also old and blind, she knew she had to accept.
"People in the village told me not to do it," she said in tears. "They said, 'He's blind, don't do it.' But I said, 'I have to do it. My children are sitting on soil. I have to. I am young. I have to get married.' That's it. I got married."

Within two days of the wedding she discovered not only that he had no money but that he had to beg for a living. Two months after her marriage when I came along on my moped she was still too ashamed to call him 'husband'. Now, she knew me better.

During all these discussions, Sakina never mentioned Tehran and the revolution. It had little to do with her life: no government had provided solutions.

On my return to Tehran, I was shocked to find that a friend had been imprisoned apparently for photographing some riots. It was frightening because none of his friends and family knew in which prison he was, how long he would be there, or whether he might be tortured. People had disappeared into prison for five, ten, fifteen years.

All the stops were pulled out to try and get him released. It was not a question of approaching organisations or institutions or courts of law; it was entirely a matter of contacting individuals. A close friend of the family knew the new military governor of Tehran; another knew someone high up in SAVAK (the secret intelligence agency); yet another achieved access to one of the prisons. A bit of manoeuvring, a bit of bribing, and the information was let slip that, yes, he'd been there that morning, but he'd been moved to another prison. Nothing more was forthcoming.

Two days later he was released. It seemed he was being transferred by bus to another prison when the man in charge called the driver to stop and told my friend to get out. He jumped off the bus in disbelief, hitched a lift home, and walked in the door laughing.

It taught me a lesson on the workings of power, and it explained why no group could unite effectively. It was individual power that mattered. The prime minister, senior army officers, university chancellors, top secret intelligence agents—all were appointed personally by the Shah, and all were removed from office at the command of the Shah. As far as I could make out, the Shah was a master manoeuvrer. He used individuals rather than institutions to support his power, while ensuring a constant fluidity and rivalry in political appointments around him. No one person was ever allowed to emerge in competition: Ayatullah Khumaini, the religious leader, was exiled; Bakhtiar, the head of SAVAK, was exiled and then killed; Arsanjani, the master-mind of Land Reform, was removed from public office and his name wiped out from most Iranian books; Mosaddeq was defeated. Hoveyda, his premier for thirteen years, presented no competitive threat. Only his twin-sister, Princess Ashraf, maintained a lasting power, but

181

then her power was linked to the power of the Shah. And *his* power was supported by oil revenues, the Western powers, the Iranian armed forces with their billions of dollars of armaments, a pervasive system of secret surveillance, and groups within Iranian society that benefited from his regime.

The restraints in Iran on individual power are limited. Parliament, the universities, the judiciary, were instituted this century and have variable independence; the tribes have lost political power; even the army lacks cohesion, for it was built by the Shah and his father as almost a personal tool with money from oil and U.S. aid. The bazaar, of course, is effective, and the mullas to some degree when they can reach agreement. But in a society subjected to change and uncertainty, it is the individual who must survive, by adapting and assimilating, by building personal contacts and networks and family links that survive the vagaries of power. The army, the religious classes, the bureaucracy, all provide the means to power; but in the end it is dangerous for an individual to ally himself to any one group or institution. An institution can always be banned or dismantled, and its members clearly identified.

On September 16th, 1978, an earthquake destroyed the desert town of Tabas and its surrounding villages in the eastern part of Iran. Within seconds, thousands of people were dead: estimates ranged from 15,000-20,000.

Help poured in, from individuals and organisations. The powers also moved in. Government aid took the shape of tents, soldiers, blankets, medicines, and tinned food; the religious leaders sent lorryloads of clothing, shoes, food, paraffin stoves, even opium for the addicts; the National Iranian Oil Company distributed free cooking paraffin every day.

I went to Tabas two weeks after the earthquake. It was shattering. The fruit and palm trees remained intact but every house had collapsed; there were piles of rubble everywhere; and intimate remnants of people's lives were scattered through the ruins.

The conditions had been appalling, with the desert heat, rotting corpses, looters, lack of fresh food and water, lack of communication. It was made worse by rivalry between the army and the religious leaders. Each antagonised the other; each ignored the

Index

Index

Index